REACHING FOR
REMARKABLE

THE 7 KEY SIGNATURES
BEHIND EVERY
REMARKABLE TEAM

TIM FOOT

LUCIDBOOKS

CONTENTS

INTRODUCTION

INTRODUCTION

"The strength of the team is each individual member.
The strength of each member is the team."
– Phil Jackson

Remarkable people can do remarkable things.

Climbers who summit Everest today overcome unimaginable challenges, following in the bold footsteps of Hillary and Norgay, who first reached the world's highest peak in 1953.

Dr. Tu Youyou combined modern science with ancient Chinese herbs to create a malaria treatment and earned a Nobel Prize for her breakthrough.

Jessica Watson was only 16 when she sailed her 34-foot yacht around the world . . . by herself.

J. R. R. Tolkien invented new worlds and languages for his beloved hobbits and kings.

Beethoven composed his *Ninth Symphony* despite being completely deaf.

Remarkable people can do remarkable things.

Yet, there is something I find even more remarkable.

What has always intrigued me most is what happens when a group of uniquely gifted contributors come together, united by a shared mission, to create something greater than anyone could achieve alone.

The team who worked tirelessly to bring the Apollo 13 astronauts safely home: the mission was survival.

The team of underdogs in the 1980 Miracle on Ice who shocked the Soviets: the mission was belief in the impossible.

The team of Allied forces who stormed the beaches of Normandy: the mission was freedom itself.

Every one of these missions was important.

Yet, none of these missions could have been accomplished by one person. They were only possible because of a team united around what mattered most.

Over the years, I've had the privilege of walking alongside leaders and teams in organizations of every kind and size. In my role as the leader of Slingshot Group, I've had a front row seat to experience and observe thousands of organizations we've served.

From start-ups to established organizations, I've seen patterns emerge and repeat that transform teams from functional to remarkable.

I've seen a consistent pathway that every team has to walk, key areas they need to focus on, and I've observed traps along the way that hold them back.

This perspective has shaped my deep conviction.

Every remarkable mission needs a remarkable team.

If you're reading this, I suspect you already carry a deep commitment to your mission. It is certainly something that fuels your passion, pulls you forward, maybe even keeps you up at night.

These pages are about turning that passion into lasting impact. I've observed there are seven key areas that remarkable teams focus on to move their mission forward. I call them the "seven signatures." I'll tell you why, but more importantly I'll show you what they are. Together we'll explore what these teams do differently, and the traps they have to overcome.

That's my promise.

Are you curious?

Let me show you how your team can start **reaching for remarkable**.

CHAPTER 1
FAST ALONE.
FAR TOGETHER.

Chapter 1

FAST ALONE.
FAR TOGETHER.

"If you want to go fast, go alone.
If you want to go far, go together."

— *African Proverb*

For as long as I can remember, I was never the fastest, nor the smartest in the room. In fact, raised by educators in the school system in Australia, I probably didn't meet the 'scholastic potential' people expected.

The first clue came when I took an IQ test in elementary school (or "primary school," as we called it in my corner of the world). I didn't score well at all. My mother, who worked at the school, was asked if she was concerned about my results.

Her response was: "Nah, he's good with people."

My mom spoke trajectory into my life that day. She foreshadowed what we now recognize as one of the key components of leadership survival in today's world: emotional intelligence (EI), also known as EQ, or "good with people."

Fast forward twenty years to a lake in The Ozarks in Missouri, where my team leader at the time had us on his ski boat shortly after I relocated stateside.

"I'll teach you to ski," Rick declared in front of my new friends, seemingly oblivious to my visible lack of upper body strength.

"I get everybody up out of the water," he continued confidently.

About 45 minutes and 13 laborious, unsuccessful attempts later, as my aching body was hauled back into the boat, he concluded:

"Well, you're good with people."

Those prophetic words repeated in my life became a label that started my understanding: to go far, I was going to have to "go together."

As I grew older, my fascination and curiosity about people grew exponentially.

I became an obsessive question-asker, and I'm still that way today. When I say obsessive, I'm not exaggerating! I used to drive my family crazy. My sons still say, "Dad, you ask too many questions!" And I respond, "Well, I'm interested. I'm curious!" And frankly, I intend to stay that way.

This curiosity led me to explore more adventurous, unpredictable paths. I had been accepted to the Tasmanian Conservatorium of Music, a decision that would have taken my life in a very different direction, but I deferred my placement for a year.

Instead, I ventured to the mainland of Australia, to "The Big Smoke," where I took on a part-time role leading the Music Department at a church on Sydney's Lower North Shore. The Senior Pastor was taking a chance on this kid from Tasmania who asked a lot of questions.

I also bi-vocationally started working in the music industry as an entertainer, along with a production assistant job at a local corporate video production house. I quickly found myself juggling more work than I could handle and had to choose opportunities that most closely fit my internal filter.

I had to ask tough questions of myself.

> What am I good at?
> What am I *not* good at?
> What drains me?
> What gives me life?

I firmly believe that we are always being prepared for what's next in our careers, and that next step is often the culmination of our experiences up until a given transition.

Ready to move to the other side of the world?

After nine years in Sydney, the sum of my experiences led me to an unexpected move: an offer to join the leadership team at LifeBridge Church in Longmont, Colorado.

I had been working at a city church with a congregation of several hundred, and now I was moving across hemispheres, countries, and cultures to work at a church of several thousand. Despite not having actively pursued this change, I felt a strong sense of "calling."

From experience, I now equate the strength of that calling with the size of the task at hand. This was a large-scale team-building project in a large organization, and looking back, I realize I couldn't have done it without every day, hour, and minute of the experiences that led me to that point.

When I asked a trusted friend if he thought I was up to the task, he wisely reminded me: "It depends on who you surround yourself with."

Coming from a smaller organization where I empowered volunteer leadership, I was well prepared to build a staff team. But it doesn't stop there. It's not just about being equipped to build a team of leaders; it's about letting them lead.

If I had tried to carry the weight myself, things might have been functional at best, lots of activity and busy work, but not much room for anything remarkable to emerge. But when our team at LifeBridge leaned in together, something different happened.

Our team was productive, healthy, relationally tight, and always evolving. Much of that came from a team-building philosophy shaped by my experiences, especially my musical ones. My most formative moments weren't when I was the strongest on the stage, they were when I was the weakest but still leading the band.

Those seasons stretched me more than anything else and quietly formed how I grew and would lead teams. It was in those early years that I realized that I get better, and we all get better, when we maximize and celebrate each other's strengths and abilities. I also began to see patterns that separate functional teams from truly remarkable ones.

The leader doesn't have to be the strongest—just the most secure.

When you allow yourself not to be the smartest person in the room or the most talented in the circle, something shifts. You grow. You learn. You make space for others to bring their best. That posture doesn't diminish you—it strengthens the whole.

Hold leadership loosely so others can lead boldly.

Teams reach their full potential when the leader doesn't cling tightly to the steering wheel. When the leader is bold and aware enough to declare: "why don't you drive for a bit."

When people are released to lead in their areas of expertise, their strengths start to complement—not compete with those around them and the mission moves forward, further and faster.

Surround yourself with people who are stronger than you.

I intentionally hired leaders who brought strengths I didn't have. I'd often say, "You're leading us today," or simply step back when someone naturally took the lead. Those moments created new momentum and reminded everyone that leadership isn't a title—it's a shared responsibility.

As the team goes, so goes the leader.

I've always believed my success rises and falls with the people around me. When the team thrives, the leader thrives. When the team grows, the leader grows. That's the heartbeat of remarkable team-building—and the lesson leading teams cemented in me.

As I look back on those early years, I'm struck by how these simple patterns kept resurfacing—truths I didn't invent, but rediscovered. They became the foundation of how I understand remarkable teams today.

As I reflect on these experiences, I'm reminded of T.S. Eliot's words from Little Gidding:

> *"We shall not cease from exploration,*
> *And the end of all our exploring*
> *Will be to arrive where we started*
> *And know the place for the first time."*

In many ways, my own journey has felt like a constant exploration, moving from one role to the next, building teams, and evolving along the way. And yet, every time I reach a new milestone, I realize that the essence of team building, and growth is something that feels familiar, like I've always known it, but now I understand and see it in a deeper way.

This sense of exploration and growth has brought me back to a place where I can sense my calling, and team-building philosophy more clearly than ever. The lessons I've learned are not just about moving forward; they're about returning to the basics with new eyes, as Eliot suggests. The journey has not been a straight line, but rather a series of circles that bring me back to where I started, each time with greater understanding.

The Start of Something New

In 2007, when two friends and mentors with complementary strengths launched Slingshot Group, a staffing and leadership coaching company, I remember wondering if this new venture would take off. It wouldn't just take off; it would further change the trajectory of my life.

In 2010, I referred a ministry to Slingshot for staffing work. Co-founder Monty Kelso invited me to jump in and actually do the work I had referred. I dipped my toe in the water, then put my whole foot in. I loved the work of building teams, figuring out what makes them healthy or unhealthy, and understanding how adding a person to a team can profoundly impact the culture and mission of an organization.

As Slingshot grew to serve thousands of ministries and faith-forward organizations, my love for this work grew too. We expanded into multiple divisions, which gave me the opportunity to lead the founding division and build out another team. This was an incredibly fulfilling experience, assembling some of the best in the field to find and coach other great leaders.

It felt like putting a band on stage with players more talented than me.

Going Together

As our work continued to scale, my focus on strategy and collaboration with organizational leaders grew as well.

Our founders invited me to take on new roles, including leading our Senior and Executive Staffing and Coaching Division and overseeing our evolving and growing Nonprofit Division. All of this culminated in an invitation to become President and CEO of Slingshot Group.

Getting to lead a team that builds, coaches, and guides other teams toward their mission was a dream.

Each and every day, I get a first-hand look at our nationwide team who is serving faith-forward organizations, churches, and nonprofits as we help them build the team their remarkable mission deserves.

We have worked in boardrooms ranging from rescue missions with small budgets and limited resources to ministry tech companies with budgets in the tens of millions. We've also worked with churches of all sizes; from those with over 30,000 members to those with fewer than 200, and everything in between.

At Slingshot, we don't just work with clients; we walk with partners. That trusted partnership approach to team-building has led to over 60% of our staffing and coaching coming from returning partners.

We've learned that an open role on a team represents both a significant opportunity and real challenges. Through our experience, we've discovered what it takes to act swiftly, confidently coach leaders to achieve breakthroughs, or fill the open role, all while propelling the mission forward.

Looking back on my work over the past few decades across continents, spanning media, music, the local church, nonprofit and for-profit ventures, staffing, and coaching, one consistent theme emerges. That theme is team: Growing them. Complementing them. Scaling them. Entrusting them. Leading them. In short, I love building teams because I've seen the power of what they can achieve that individuals simply can't.

That's why the African proverb rings so true:

> *"If you want to go fast, go alone. If you want to go far,*
> *go together."*

Missions don't move because one person is brilliant; they move because people commit, align, and do the work together.

> If your mission matters, your team matters more.
> If you want to start reaching for remarkable, don't go alone. Go together.

How far will your mission take you? Let's talk about that next.

CHAPTER 2
YOUR MISSION IS NOT ENOUGH

Chapter 2

YOUR MISSION IS NOT ENOUGH

"It's not enough to have a good team.
The team has to row in the same direction."

—*Warren Buffet*

What's your mission statement?

Most leaders can answer that question quickly. Some can even recite it by heart. And for good reason—a clear mission is the heartbeat of a team. It unites people around a cause that matters, a "why" that propels them forward.

Companies frame missions around world-shaping ideas:

- **United Airlines**: "Connect people and unite the world."

- **Microsoft**: "To empower every person and every organization on the planet to achieve more."

- **Google**: "To organize the world's information and make it universally accessible and useful."

Nonprofits do this even more boldly:

- **The Nature Conservancy**: "To conserve the lands and waters on which all life depends."

- **charity: water**: "We're on a mission to bring clean and safe drinking water to every person on the planet."

- **Habitat for Humanity**: "Seeking to put God's love into action, Habitat for Humanity brings people together to build homes, communities, and hope."

A good mission transforms practical endeavors, like building homes, into something far greater: building hope. Who doesn't want to build hope?

Churches, more than any other organization, exemplify how to express one mission in a million different ways. That mission is simple: "To make disciples."

"Therefore go and make disciples of all nations, baptizing them in the name of the Father and of the Son and of the Holy Spirit, and teaching them to obey everything I have commanded you" (Matthew 28:19-20a).

In all my years of serving, leading, and investing in the local church, (which I continue to do today, I consider it the highest calling and privilege) I've seen the power of a remarkable mission being powered by remarkable teams. I've also seen the challenges, have seen leadership falter and fail and the struggle that comes from human interactions— the traps that so easily undermine progress. But, I have also seen the resilience and beauty of a mission that has endured for thousands of years and promises eternal impact.

But again, the mission alone is never enough.

A Surprising Discovery

I've lost count of how many inspiring mission statements I've read, engraved on boardroom walls, featured prominently on websites, or printed in glossy brochures. The mission was there.

Bold. Visionary. Clear.

Did that remarkable mission guarantee success? Unfortunately, not.

Churches have closed their doors even while maintaining the deepest dedication to the mission.

Despite their needed and noble purpose, nonprofit organizations have failed to reach their full potential leading to struggles in achieving their goals and eventual closure.

Take Hull House, for example. It became one of the United States' most significant pioneer social service organizations when Jane Addams and Ellen Gates Starr established it in

Chicago in 1889. The mission of the organization promised "to provide assistance to individuals in need and to promote social change through education, healthcare, and community activities."

During its more than 100-year existence, Hull House served as a key provider of essential services to struggling immigrant communities. During its initial years, Hull House led efforts which resulted in the passage of groundbreaking laws that protected women and children from workplace abuse. The advocacy from Hull House established its path as a leader in national reforms that protected both American workers and vulnerable children.

Hull House ended its operations in 2012 because financial difficulties made it impossible to continue. The organization's essential mission should not have been undermined to the point of financial collapse.

The organization folded after neglecting its internal management problems for an extended period. This snapshot demonstrates powerfully that an extraordinary mission alone does not guarantee organizational longevity.

Speaking of snapshots, remember Kodak cameras which captured childhood memories for generations? Can you recall what it felt like to hold the camera? Developing film required winding it forward, taking it to a Kodak store for processing and then waiting eagerly to see your photos in a Kodak envelope that included negatives to examine under the light.

Despite attempts to venture into digital imaging and printers, Kodak couldn't compete with more agile and innovative competitors like Canon and Sony. By the time Kodak finally embraced digital photography, many other companies had already dominated the digital camera market. Kodak's offerings couldn't catch up. Not to mention the amazing cameras we now carry in our back pockets and constantly have in our hands. It seems the number one feature on any new release of Apple's iPhone is usually the improved quality and capabilities of its camera.

Here's a surprising stat: The number of photographs captured in one minute during present times in the United States surpasses the total photographs taken throughout the entire 19th century. Within one year today we take more photos than the total number captured throughout the 20th century.

Kodak's story is a classic tale of innovation stagnation and strategic missteps, illustrating how even industry giants can fail if they don't stay ahead of changing technological trends.

Their final mission statement before they filed bankruptcy was: "To make photography easy and accessible for everyone."

Are you getting the message? A remarkable mission is not enough. You need a remarkable team.

Can we learn from cautionary tales like Kodak and Hull House and teams you know who fell short of accomplishing their mission?

Could it be that there's a consistent path that every team must take to reach for remarkable?

There is.

Key Signatures

Early in my musical journey, I realized something surprising: the best, and even the worst, songs you've ever heard all begin the same way. Not with a melody. Not with a lyric. But with a framework.

Every song travels a defined route before it ever reaches your ears—a journey that shapes where it can go and what it can become. That pathway determines which notes belong, how the song feels, and how the players move together. In music, that pathway is marked by the Key Signature. There are seven of them—seven starting points that give every song its identity and direction.

A key signature doesn't limit the music; it frees it. It sets the rails the musicians run on, creating harmony, unity, and shared understanding. It's the invisible guide that makes improvisation possible and creativity sustainable. Without it, even the most talented players would drift out of tune, clash in tone, or compete for space. With it, they create something cohesive, powerful, and sometimes . . . unforgettable.

What if, similar to signatures in music, there are key signatures that guide the most remarkable teams?

I'm confident and convinced that there are.

And that's where the 7 *Key Signatures* behind every remarkable team comes in.

The seven key signatures behind every remarkable team

Just as key signatures chart the pathway for a song, there are key signatures that chart the pathway for a team. Every team you've ever been part of—unhealthy, inconsistent, functional, or truly remarkable—is traveling the same pathway. It's the pathway every team must navigate to accomplish its mission. These 7 key signatures are likely familiar to all of us, yet are so often overlooked.

- **Conviction**—A clear and shared sense of why you exist and what you're called to do.
- **Message**—A compelling and consistent way of communicating what matters most.
- **Culture**—Values and behaviors that shape the soul of your team.
- **Roles**—Unique contributions for remarkable impact.
- **Systems**—Scalable design for remarkable growth.
- **Friction**—Embracing healthy conflict for growth.
- **Risk**—Bold moves that drive remarkable learnings and outcomes.

In this book, I will share what I have learned from leading, building, and working with thousands of teams. These seven form a compelling pathway that moves teams from functional to remarkable. This vital pathway promotes strengths, and the power of collaboration. These seven signatures provide constructs to adapt, change, and move forward together with shared understanding. And as the team moves forward so does the mission which most importantly becomes a co-mission.

How LEGO Rebuilt Their Mission

LEGO is a fantastic example of all seven of these signatures in action.

If you grew up in the last century, chances are you remember the joy of LEGO: hours on the floor, bricks scattered everywhere, building towers, castles, or starships. For many of us, LEGO wasn't just toy building blocks; they were a gateway to creativity and imagination. Generation Alpha almost never knew that joy.

By the 2000s, the brand synonymous with childhood fun and activity for generations was on the verge of bankruptcy. The company had lost its **conviction** and lost its way, following too many trends (theme parks, clothing lines, video games, etc.), and lacked any clear sense of purpose. Recovery began when LEGO rediscovered its conviction: to inspire and develop the builders of tomorrow. With their heartbeat revived, LEGO could be true to its **message**.

Instead of saying, "We make toys," LEGO began to tell a story parents, kids, and educators could get behind: the importance of unleashing creativity and imagination.

Clarifying the mission meant clarifying the **roles**. Under new leadership, LEGO cut the excess, reorganized the teams, and empowered designers and engineers to contribute to the mission in their own unique ways. A bloated, complacent **culture** was replaced with one that celebrated creativity and disciplined innovation. At the same time, the **systems** needed an overhaul. LEGO standardized production got costs under control and built new systems that served—not distracted from—the mission. And they had to face the healthy **friction** they had long ignored. The hard decisions of closing theme parks and cutting bloated operations forced LEGO to take a long, hard look at what wasn't working instead of sweeping it under the rug.

Finally, LEGO took on **risk**. Not the reckless, desperate risk that many companies try when their backs are against the wall, but rather smart, bold, strategic risks. LEGO's partnerships with Hollywood (LEGO Star Wars and Harry Potter), their forays into digital-first strategies, and even their launch of LEGO Ideas (a platform that allowed fans to submit and vote on new sets) were game-changers. Each risk was intentional and tied back to LEGO's core conviction and message.

A lack of conviction, muddled message, unclear roles, complacent culture, sloppy systems, fear of friction, and reckless risk are what nearly caused LEGO to derail from functional to total demise. What revived LEGO was the pathway of these seven signatures in powerful ways. Their transformation wasn't just a business case study; it was an organizational example of what happens when a team moves beyond functional and starts reaching for remarkable.

Self-Awareness vs. Team Awareness

Self-awareness is one of the most celebrated traits in leadership—and rightly so. Every remarkable leader knows the importance of understanding their strengths, naming their blind spots, and recognizing the patterns that shape how they show up. Self-awareness helps a leader clarify conviction, articulate a message, live out values, and steward their own role with humility and confidence. It's why entire shelves of leadership books are dedicated to personality assessments, emotional intelligence, and reflective practices. Self-awareness matters. But it's only half the story.

The quiet villain in many organizations isn't a lack of self-awareness—it's the absence of team awareness. Leaders can be incredibly self-aware and still be oblivious to how their team is experiencing the seven signatures. They may feel personally aligned in conviction, while their team is unclear on why they exist. They may believe the message is consistent, while their team hears mixed signals. A leader may be intentional about culture, but the team may be living in a very different reality. Leaders often understand their role, but struggle to see the role clarity (or confusion) around them. They trust the systems they've put in place, unaware those systems frustrate or slow down others. They may welcome friction and risk for themselves, but fail to recognize how their team avoids, fears, or mismanages both.

This is why teams get stuck in functional mode. Leaders assume that personal clarity equals organizational clarity, but those are not the same thing.

Self-awareness is about knowing yourself; team awareness is about knowing how the whole team is navigating these seven signatures.

That's why our Team Awareness Assessment (more on this later in the book) uses a simple sliding scale:

Unhealthy → Inconsistent → Functional → Remarkable

This assessment helps to reveal where a team truly stands. A leader might believe their conviction is remarkable, while the team experiences it as inconsistent. They may think systems are functional, while the team feels they're unhealthy bottlenecks. These gaps aren't about blame; they're about clarity.

Remarkable teams aren't built on one person's clarity. If we want to reach for remarkable, we have to be honest about where we all are right now. Self-awareness gets a leader started, but team awareness shows the whole team the path forward. You can't chart a remarkable future until you know your present reality.

Are you reaching for remarkable?

In the upcoming chapters, we'll define and dig into the seven signatures that define remarkable teams to increase your "team awareness," harness dissonance, and create harmony that will propel your team and mission forward. Along the way, we'll acknowledge the traps that distract us from focusing on the very elements that propel our teams and missions forward.

So, here's my challenge to you:

> Reach for remarkable. The mission you're pursuing is too important, the stakes too high, and the people around you too valuable to aim for anything less.

I truly believe that we are facing a crisis in leadership. A crisis where burnout, breakdowns, meltdowns, and isolation are all too common, leading to toxic and narcissistic leadership tendencies.

Healthy and remarkable are rare, but they don't have to be. When teams focus on these seven signatures, they can create collective impact, making the world, or at least their corner of it, a better place.

To truly understand the benefits and features of remarkable teams that are healthy in each of these key signatures, you need to do more than read; you need to put these principles into practice and watch them unfold in your own team's context.

Your remarkable mission doesn't just need this, it deserves this! Let's dig into the Seven Signatures and reach for remarkable together.

CHAPTER 3
CONVICTION

CHAPTER 3

SIGNATURE #1 CONVICTION

A clear and shared sense of why you exist and what you're called to do.

"People don't buy what you do, they buy why you do it."

—Simon Sinek

On December 3, 1903, the New York Times wrote, "A man-carrying airplane will eventually be built, but only if mathematicians and engineers work steadily for the next ten million years."

Ten. Million. Years.

At the time, it seemed reasonable.

Alexander Graham Bell, the inventor of the telephone, also tried to solve the flight problem. However, his lack of a practical design and hands-on approach, combined with an unconventional mindset, limited his success. Despite assembling a talented team, they struggled to find a viable solution.

Thomas Edison, famous for the incandescent light bulb, also aspired to invent human flight. However, his focus was scattered, and his teams often lacked the depth of knowledge or research needed to take flight. Edison's tendency to work either alone or with small, less-experienced teams hindered his ability to innovate in this area.

It makes me wonder, did their past successes as inventors make them overconfident? Did they get trapped by their own theories, believing past achievements would automatically translate to success in the air? And when the challenge shifted, were they unable to pivot in the ways needed to crack the flight code?

When you stack up the long list of failures—from the famous to the forgotten—it's easy to see why the New York Times felt so certain. Ten million years felt like a safe bet. If the greatest inventors at the time couldn't get us off the ground, why would anyone else?

Just ten days after that headline predicting humanity was ten million years away from flight, the Wright brothers proved the world wrong and, for the first time in human history, flew a powered airplane.

In that moment, the course of history shifted, and the world would never be the same.

While it seemed that everyone else viewed the idea of a man-carrying airplane as impossible, the Wright Brothers were convicted otherwise.

Behind their remarkable conviction was a remarkable team: a team driven by the same mission and values.

The Wright brothers and their team were fully committed to advancing the science of flight. Their conviction about their ability to solve any problem that arose on their journey was steadfast. They had the clarity and resilience to push through external pressures and fierce competition, all with one goal: to fly.

> ## Key Signature #1
>
> Conviction: A clear and shared sense of why you exist and what you're called to do

A remarkable team filters everything and everyone through its deeply held convictions.

Is conviction intuitive? I used to think so. As I've led teams and observed the most remarkable ones, I've seen time and time again that it requires deliberate effort. Remarkable teams don't just talk about their mission, they use their core conviction to filter their actions, decisions, and relationships.

It's one thing to post your mission statement on the wall or include it in your annual report, but it's another to talk about it in a way that inspires your team to live it out.

The Wright brothers and their team's commitment to flight and their conviction that it was possible led them to understand the four forces of flight: lift, weight, drag, and thrust. They weren't just dreaming; they were making the dream a reality.

A balanced commitment to these forces is essential for success.

These forces may help provide a framework as we unpack our first key signature of a remarkable team.

Conviction serves as the necessary starting point on our pathway to remarkable, providing the "lift" we need as we harness the power of purpose.

In *Start With Why*, author Simon Sinek warns that many teams obsess over what they do and overlook why they do it. His famous reminder: "People don't buy what you do, they buy why you do it." This underscores a simple truth: conviction is born from clarity of purpose.

Remarkable teams are grounded in a clear conviction about their identity. Identity determines function—knowing who we are clarifies why we do what we do and the unique role we play. In flight terms, conviction is the thrust that powers clarity. Without it, a team loses direction. We see this time and again in the marketplace especially when facing big decisions, critical decisions like choosing which type of aircraft to fly, deciding when to close over 3,000 stores, or determining where to open new locations. Conviction also guides teams when to pivot from failed experiments and chart new ways to soar.

Purpose provides the necessary lift to a team's conviction on the path to remarkable, but it's balanced by the weight of clarity and self-definition.

The Power of Conviction

Conviction shows up in surprising places, even in the fast-food world, where two companies are driven by something far deeper than food.

Let's start with Chick-fil-A, whose purpose has guided them from the beginning:

> *"To glorify God by being a faithful steward of all that is entrusted to us. To have a positive influence on all who come in contact with Chick-fil-A."*

At first glance, it's surprising to see a fast-food chain anchored to a purpose like that. But for the faith-forward Cathy family, this isn't just a line on a wall—it's the center of who they are and why they exist. And like all real conviction, it comes with a cost.

Their sense of identity has remained unwavering, and they've become incredibly successful without compromising their convictions. One example is their decision to close on Sundays to observe a day of rest and allow their team to worship. This decision has sparked controversy, with some states even attempting to legislate against it. Chick-fil-A remains closed on Sundays, and their earnings have only grown stronger as a result of their conviction.

Why stay closed on Sunday when they are leaving millions on the table? Conviction.

In a similar vein, In-N-Out Burger's mission statement is clear:

"Providing the freshest, highest quality foods and services for a profit and a spotless, sparkling environment whereby the customer is our most important asset."

That conviction has a cost too. This strong conviction has led them to hold on store expansions in areas where they can't maintain their high standards of quality. They refuse to sacrifice their commitment to freshness, even if it limits growth, and it has earned them unmatched brand respect.

If you turn over their soda cups, you'll find a clue as to where their identity and conviction come from: John 3:16 is printed on the bottom. This conviction has also driven their extensive nonprofit work, including the In-N-Out Burger Foundation, which focuses on preventing child abuse and neglect, and the Slave 2 Nothing Foundation, which fights against substance abuse and human trafficking. We've had the privilege of partnering with them to find staff, inspired by their mission-driven work.

Southwest Airlines gives us another interesting picture of conviction in action. Their purpose has long been clear:

"To connect people to what's important in their lives through friendly, reliable, and low-cost air travel."

Southwest once led the way in low-cost air travel, and their conviction drove bold decisions like standardizing their fleet, their open seating boarding policy, and "Bags always fly free" . . . ahem, bags flew free! Southwest at time of writing is an interesting case study of convictions changing or evolving. Organizations are constantly tested. Markets shift. Costs rise. Passengers complain. Competitors innovate. And for Southwest seat allocation and bag fees are now a reality as they continue to innovate in other ways. Convictions can change. Sometimes they need to.

Conviction Traps

Conviction is the foundation of organizational clarity. It points the way and fuels the will to move. But even a team with strong conviction must manage the forces that press against forward motion. Think like a pilot. Flight depends on a live balance of lift, weight, drag, and thrust. Teams face the same mix. When clarity slips, when side work swallows focus, when alignment frays, the plane drifts off course. As your team fights for conviction, you should also avoid these traps.

The Confusion Trap

When you're stuck in the confusion trap, clarity slips away, purpose gets fuzzy, values drift, and the team's energy starts to scatter.

When a team hasn't clearly defined its purpose, mission, and values, belief may still be present, but direction is not.

Without a shared why, people start operating from their own assumptions, decisions lose their filter, communication drifts, and momentum inevitably slows.

Confusion often comes from mistaking belief for conviction. Belief says the words, but conviction carries weight and direction. Conviction will cost you something, and grows when the why is concrete and lived out.

This work is delicate. Spend all your time in abstract purpose work and you drift into talk without traction. Spend too little time and you get thin belief that cannot lift the work. The goal is a clear, purposeful "why" supported by lived and shared stories that make that why visible.

Here are a few steady helpful habits:

- Name the goal in one sentence.
- Tie it to why it matters now.
- State the next step, the owner, and the date.
- Invite your team to repeat back what they heard.
- Listen.
- Celebrate the right behaviors.
- Prune work that does not serve the core.
- Realign with stakeholders on a regular rhythm.
- Show the changes that came from those conversations.

Do these small things on purpose. You will avoid confusion, resist drift, and repair misalignment before it grows. The team stays on mission. The mission moves forward.

Want to help others share in your team's conviction? Tell stories. Don't just recite a mission statement and hope belief turns into conviction. Gather your people and let the mission take shape through true stories and in real scenes. Our team has met on a beach to talk about waves and momentum. We once met in an airplane hangar to explore the forces of flight and how they mirror our work. We rode jeeps and hiked through a forest to learn from an Aspen grove where each tree is connected to the next. These moments, tied to stories of lives, families, and organizations changed, fertilize conviction. They turn words into work and will into power.

Celebrate the behaviors you want repeated, especially the unseen ones. Quiet excellence signals what matters and reinforces the mission without a lecture. Over time, confusion gives way to shared language, and shared language gives way to shared action.

Purpose lifts. Focus reduces drag. Clarity and alignment balances the weight of the work across the whole team. When these three work together, conviction grows and results follow.

The Drift Trap

Side projects pull attention from the main thing because the why is not actively guarded.

Even the clearest teams begin to wander when the why is not kept in view. New ideas show up, side efforts start to multiply, and good work slowly edges out the right work. Drift rarely feels dangerous in the moment. It feels interesting. It sounds urgent. But over time it pulls energy away from the center and leads to distraction.

Guard the main thing in simple ways.

- Keep a short statement of purpose in every planning space.

- Begin meetings or gatherings by naming the aim in one sentence.

- Tie each initiative back to mission and values. If the tie is weak, pause it or prune it. That choice feeds conviction because it shows that purpose is more than talk.

Use memorable environments and shared experiences to renew focus. The beach, the hangar, the forest. Each setting gave us a picture that endures, and each picture keeps the center in view when busy seasons tempt us to scatter. Add celebration to that rhythm. Point to a teammate who lived the mission when no one was watching. Tell that story. It pulls attention back to what matters most.

Drift is not a strategy problem first. It is a stewardship problem. You steward attention by returning again and again to the why and by letting the why shape what you start, what you stop, and what you sustain.

The Misalignment Trap

When teams skip regular realignment with stakeholders, choices and values stop matching.

Alignment does not persist on its own. People change. Conditions shift. Assumptions harden. Without scheduled realignment, small gaps become costly detours. Work begins to look right on paper but wrong to the people who matter most.

Realignment is simple and human.

- Meet with key stakeholders.
- Rehearse purpose and values in plain words.
- Review what you are doing and why it fits.
- Ask what no longer fits.
- Ask who no longer fits.
- Confirm the next few moves, the owners, and the dates.
- Close the loop with what you heard and what you changed.

Research has long noted that teams who revisit purpose with stakeholders show higher engagement and lower burnout than those who do not. The practice is worth the calendar space.

Think of this as flight control. Instruments must be read. Headings must be corrected. Weather must be noted. In team life, the instruments are purpose, values, goals, and the lived stories that confirm them. These instruments determine the temperature of the team and whether the air will be smooth or choppy.

Read them together. Adjust together. Move forward together.

Conviction Priorities

Conviction is a driving force that propels your team forward. Without it, a team can drift aimlessly, no matter how compelling the mission may seem. But having strong convictions doesn't just happen, it requires intentional effort and clarity.

Here are three common myths about conviction that prevent your team from the kind of deep-rooted commitment that leads to extraordinary results.

Priority #1—Clarity Work

Many teams believe that their remarkable mission is enough (and this is a primary reason for the writing of this book). Many think the mission is so compelling that it will naturally create convicted disciples. This is absolutely a myth. In fact, studies in organizational psychology show that intentional effort is required to articulate and align a team's convictions. This is why I took our team to the beach, the airfield, and the forest—to actively engage in defining and reinforcing our shared purpose.

I'm sure the Wright brothers spent a lot of time dreaming together and with their team about the possibility of flight.

Patrick Lencioni, in his book *The Five Dysfunctions of a Team*, highlights that ambiguity around team values leads to a lack of commitment and weak accountability. Without deliberate effort, teams often operate based on assumed or conflicting values.[1] Lencioni argues that ambiguity within a team, especially regarding values, roles, and goals, undermines trust and commitment.

Without clarity, team members are less likely to take ownership, leading to weak accountability and misaligned efforts. He emphasizes that teams must intentionally define their shared convictions and priorities to avoid the confusion and dysfunction that ambiguity breeds.

Priority #2—Team Alignment

Don't buy into the myth that by simply hiring the right leaders, they will naturally bleed for the mission. "We shouldn't need to sit around the fire singing Kumbaya." While I'm not suggesting a fireside sing-along (but who doesn't like a good one?! Especially with those who can't sing), this attitude is risky. Teams often hesitate to engage in self-definition exercises because they perceive them as

---

[1] Lencioni, Patrick. *The Five Dysfunctions of a Team: A Leadership Fable*. 10th anniversary ed., Jossey-Bass, 2012, 207-209.

distractions from "real work." This perception overlooks the productivity gains that come from alignment.

Research by Gallup shows that teams aligned with clear core convictions experience 29% higher profitability and 72% lower employee turnover.[2]

This statistic on turnover should have you scheduling a brainstorm right now about how to deepen conviction in your team. Turnover is one of the biggest threats to mission momentum.

Priority #3—Internal Commitment

External measures of success (e.g., KPIs, customer reviews, or rankings) are often mistaken for the lift that propels conviction, but in reality, they can be the weight that drags an organization down during times of retraction following growth or flat years.

Letting external measures or results drive conviction puts you at the mercy of the metrics rather than fully committing to the mission itself. This is why true conviction cannot be built on external validation. It must come from within, anchored in the team's shared values, purpose, and vision.

---

[2] "How to Create a Strengths-Based Company Culture." *Gallup CliftonStrengths*, Gallup, https://www.gallup.com/clifton strengths/en/290903/how-to-create-strengths-based-company-culture.aspx.

In the end, moving from belief to conviction isn't just about making lofty statements or achieving short-term wins. It's about building a culture of deep-rooted commitment where everyone is aligned and energized by a shared purpose. Only when conviction is cultivated intentionally, nurtured through action, and anchored in clarity can a team truly thrive and achieve its remarkable potential. As you move forward, remember: Conviction is not just the starting point—it's the fuel that keeps your team moving forward, even (and especially) when the road gets rough.

Avoiding Drag and Mission Drift

If there had been a lack of conviction for the Wright Brothers, we might still be waiting ten million years to fly. Chick-fil-A would have compromised its identity by opening on Sundays, and In-N-Out would have lost its unwavering commitment to quality which sets it apart.

The weighty work of self-definition, balanced with the lift that comes from active commitment to clarity, is crucial to your journey toward building a team defined by conviction.

But even with strong conviction, there is always the risk of drag, forces that can slow down progress when a team fails to regularly revisit its core convictions. Time, money, resources, and valuable energy are lost when we don't pause to ask the critical questions:

Who are we?
Why do we exist?
What is our unique contribution?

These questions prevent drag and mission drift. They help clarify the evolving nature of an organization's remarkable mission and deepen a team's commitment to it. When asked consistently, these questions become part of the ethos of all you do, and they start to be instinctively and naturally applied when evaluating initiatives.

This creates a filter for deciding whether new ideas align with the mission or are just distractions:

Is this who we are?
Does this reflect why we exist?
Is this in line with our unique contribution?

Without a commitment to this kind of clarity, you will experience unnecessary drag that slows or even stalls your progress. This kind of drag can present as:

- Trying to juggle innovation with short-term demands from various stakeholders.

- Lacking clarity on whether your focus should be on disruptive innovation or incremental improvements.

- Experiencing communication breakdowns between teams and organizational leaders.

This all requires alignment through dialogue and collaboration. To many leaders, this will feel like unnecessary drag that slows momentum. I would argue that sometimes we need to slow down to go faster. In fact, the drag of this process can stop us from overshooting the runway and crashing the plane. The Wright Brothers were certainly onto something when they recognized that drag is just as critical as lift in the forces of flight.

I can't count the number of times I've been leading a meeting and realized that if we hadn't slowed down (embracing some conversational drag), we would have absolutely crashed the plane of our mission, diving headfirst into a new initiative or innovation without the clarity and alignment we needed.

Testing and Refining Conviction

In the early days of Slingshot, we were in a meeting with a room full of strong opinions. Ideas were flying, tensions were rising, and everyone was convinced their solution was the right one. In the middle of it all, Stan, one of our co-founders, walked in a little late. He listened quietly for a moment, leaned back, folded his arms, and asked, "Has anyone here ever sat in the cockpit of an airplane?"

The room froze. David, a new team member, later admitted he thought, "Who is this guy, and why is he derailing this conversation?"

But Stan was not derailing anything. He was re-centering us. He always had a unique ability to point us back to purpose through stories and metaphors. This one was inspired by his late father Lyle who was a Hellcat fighter pilot in the Navy during World War II. After the war, young pilots at his local regional airport considered him their version of Chuck Yeager (a famous pilot who embodied his own conviction in the aviation industry).

Right there in the meeting, Stan explained the cockpit instruments and how every gauge works together to help a pilot determine direction, altitude, and speed. By the time he finished, the debate we were having suddenly made sense. We were arguing about details without agreeing on direction. His metaphor clarified the issue, and the decision fell easily into place.

It was a simple moment that slowed us down long enough to powerfully refine our conviction.

Conviction must be tested, refined, and brought back into view or a team drifts.

We've found through our staffing and coaching work that leaders are far less likely to leave when they are clear on their team's conviction and have a consistent voice through ongoing dialogue.

A crucial part of refining this key signature of conviction for your remarkable team, though it may feel like drag, is the process of testing convictions. I remember working with a team where the leader would occasionally throw out an idea that was clearly contrary to the mission of the organization to actually test the team's conviction and cause them to rally around their "why." The invaluable end-product of that exercise was "tested conviction" and closer alignment.

Studies in organizational psychology highlight the value of iterative learning. Testing convictions through small-scale experiments or pilots allows teams to validate their direction and refine their approach.

The Stanford Social Innovation Review highlights a Non-Governmental Organization (NGO) that successfully used pilot projects to ensure alignment with its mission before scaling its efforts. By testing small initiatives, the NGO was able to evaluate their impact and refine their approach, reducing the risk of resource misallocation. This iterative process allowed the organization to stay true to its mission of empowering underprivileged communities while adapting to local needs. The pilots also produced greater team cohesion, as members saw tangible evidence of their convictions in action.

Ultimately, this strategy helped the NGO achieve sustainable impact and maintain its focus on core values despite external pressures.

Perhaps Southwest Airlines experimenting with changing its proprietary boarding and open seating policy is actually part of their continued commitment to align with their missional convictions around customer satisfaction. Evidence of this being the inviting of customers into their testing phase with regular updates such as this:

> *"We have found that our boarding process allows us to board the most efficiently. We'll still line up and board quickly to get you on your way. We'll provide more details as we continue our transformation."*

Continued "transformation" is another way of saying "we're testing our convictions."

Iterative learning, pilots, and experimentation also provide leadership development opportunities as team members step up in new and innovative ways. It's also an excellent strategy for developing leaders from within and boosting their confidence through the wins and growth that come from the freedom to fail forward.

One leader I once coached described this process of innovation and experimentation as "bowling with bumpers." Eventually, the bumpers are removed as the leader grows in confidence and conviction, and the experimentation yields results—either knocking down pins or requiring realignment, which is another example of healthy drag.

However, this process can quickly become unhealthy drag if progress and learnings aren't properly documented and communicated.

Just like the rehearsal process for an orchestra or a band is in its essence "iterative," I suspect this was vital for the Wright Brothers as they learned from their "bad performances" and epic failures and also their incremental wins and moments of "lift and thrust" on the path to the first flight. I equally suspect that the stories of those who never made it off the ground lack the kind of careful documentation and reflection that would have helped them succeed.

But zooming out to clearly documented mission and vision statements is the "30,000 ft" level work that will bring focus to the details happening on the ground.

Notably, the "Journal of Business Ethics" shows that well-defined mission and vision statements significantly improve organizational alignment and decision-making. These documents provide a reference point for teams to evaluate whether their actions reflect their convictions.

We've observed that the most remarkable teams are laser-focused on their conviction. This is invariably traced back to a clear and concise mission statement that is not just a slogan or words on the wall, but one that's lived out through deeply held conviction. This conviction drives everything and becomes a vital filter for guarding against distractions. It allows remarkable teams to use the force of drag, not to slow them down, but to keep them on mission by saying no to anything that doesn't align with who they are, why they exist, and their unique contribution.

Fueling Remarkable Teams

Finally, to land the plane on the topic of conviction, it's important to understand that the benefits of a team operating with strong convictions are profound and far-reaching. Conviction provides the thrust needed for sustained focus, resilience, and success.

Let's elevate our metaphor from plane flight to rocket travel. NASA's determination to achieve the moon landing despite setbacks like the Apollo I tragedy highlights the foundational conviction that can propel teams to extraordinary heights. JFK's iconic "We Choose the Moon" speech rallied an entire nation behind a purpose that was uncertain at the time:

> *"We choose to go to the moon in this decade and do the other things, not because they are easy, but because they are hard; because that goal will serve to organize and measure the best of our energies and skills, because that challenge is one that we are willing to accept, one we are unwilling to postpone, and one we intend to win, and the others, too."*

But here's the key: Don't fall into the trap of thinking that a "me" conviction is enough. Team conviction reaches remarkable heights only when it moves from "me" to "we." Would the mission to the moon have succeeded if it had been solely JFK's vision? No.

Teams with clear "we" convictions experience the thrust of enhanced decision-making, where their values serve as a filter for strategic choices. The most remarkable teams I have observed and served are laser-focused on their convictions, saying no to everything else that doesn't align with their shared purpose.

Think again of our examples from this chapter: Southwest, Chick-fil-A, In-N-Out, and the Wright brothers. These companies and teams could only have succeeded with shared "we" convictions, convictions that aligned their efforts and propelled them toward achieving remarkable goals.

According to MIT Sloan Management Review, companies that align decision-making with core values experience higher employee engagement and customer loyalty, as consistency in actions builds trust.[3] Another example is the clothing company Patagonia, which has built its entire brand around environmental sustainability. Their commitment guides

---

[3] Aronson, Daniel. "Why It's Good for Business When Customers Share Your Values." *MIT Sloan Management Review*, 15 Feb. 2024, https://sloanreview.mit.edu/article/why-its-good-for-business-when-customers-share-your-values/

every decision, from supply chain practices to product design. For example, Patagonia's unexpected but ingenious "Don't Buy This Jacket" campaign encouraged customers to repair and reuse rather than consume unnecessarily. Despite the paradoxical message, the campaign saw increased sales (thrust) and a significant growth in brand loyalty. Patagonia's commitment created "we" convictions in their customers.

Shared conviction also provides the thrust of team cohesion and morale, leading to a sense of unity and purpose. We've seen this time and again in our work staffing and coaching ministry teams that thrive in deeper ways after aligning more closely around a shared missional focus.

The greatest inspiration for shared team conviction is ultimately Jesus and his disciples. They didn't just believe in Jesus' mission; they were so convicted by it that they committed their lives to it. They were willing to die for it and most of them did. There is no greater conviction than that!

Similarly, many of the NGOs and nonprofit organizations we work with display incredible clarity around shared "we" convictions, driven by the greater good that motivates their teams. This unwavering focus keeps them laser-focused on decisions that move their mission forward.

A study from Deloitte reveals that companies with a strong purpose experience a 30% increase in innovation capacity and adaptability compared to those that lack a defined mission. When we approach our work with a sense of higher purpose, even the toughest tasks feel more manageable, and the rewards of our accomplishments feel far more meaningful. This kind of strong shared conviction acts as a trap-proofing mechanism for teams, shielding them from distractions. The most remarkable teams are laser-focused on their conviction, saying yes to the right things and no to everything that doesn't align with who they are, why they exist, and their unique contribution.

This chapter has been packed with examples of such teams. Can you name a single team that left a meaningful mark on this earth without starting with conviction?

Here's a question for you: Do you merely believe in the mission and purpose of your team, or are you convicted by it? If you lead the team, ask your key stakeholders this question. Then follow up with: Why?

Finding the Right Team for the Right Mission

When we discover our unique conviction and contribution to the world, there's a team that needs it. That needs you! The noble pursuit is finding that remarkable team that embraces the part only you can play. Teams with strong conviction naturally attract like-minded partners, stakeholders, and supporters. This is something we emphasize constantly in organizations, advising them to tell the most compelling and convicting story about their mission in order to attract the best like-minded leaders to their teams.

Don't waste your time trying to fit into the wrong team or despairing over not being chosen (conversations we have regularly with candidates in our staffing work). Instead, invest your emotion and energy in finding, pursuing, and building up the right team. A team that journeys together with shared conviction, experiences the lift of alignment, and embraces the necessary weight and drag. This is where the true thrust of remarkable teams lies: in the power of conviction.

My friend Brian shared a story that beautifully illustrated this point for me:

> *My mentor, Joe Ritchie, holds the world record for the fastest time flying across the country in a turboprop plane. In fact, he smashed the old record, averaging more than 100 miles an hour faster.*
>
> *One morning, over coffee, I asked Joe, "What's the story about you flying across the country faster than anyone else?"*
>
> *Joe took a sip from his cup and said, "Oh, my buddy, Steve Fossett, liked collecting world records, and I had the plane to do it. Chuck Yeager had the record. When Chuck flew, he removed everything that wasn't needed for flying, and when he landed, he flew it so hard he burned up both engines."*
>
> *Joe continued, "When we took my plane, I didn't strip it, and when we landed, the engines were fine."*

I asked the obvious question: "So, how'd you do it?"

Joe took another sip, put his cup down, and said, "Tailwind."

He wasn't done and went into mentor mode. "Always look for tailwind. And the best way to find tailwind is who you choose to work with. The right people will give you tailwind."

The right people are the ones who share your "we" conviction. With the right people your team will experience the tailwind to propel you forward. Even during seasons when the winds shift, you'll have the resilience to pull together and navigate through choppy air, ultimately finding smoother skies as you revisit clarity around your vision and mission, your "why," and prioritize conviction as a cornerstone of team strategy.

When Stan walked into our meeting late that day and disrupted our conversation with a story about airplane cockpits, he was speaking about the conviction that continues to sustain us today. It was conviction that led the Wright brothers to shorten the New York Times' prediction from 10 million years to 10 days. It was their conviction that made Stan's metaphor and our constant gallivanting around the world possible.

And it's conviction that will allow your team to reach an altitude that's remarkable.

CHAPTER 4
MESSAGE

SIGNATURE #2 MESSAGE

A compelling and consistent way of communicating what matters most, because everything communicates.

"My model for business is The Beatles. They were four guys who kept each other's kind of negative tendencies in check. They balanced each other and the total was greater than the sum of the parts. That's how I see business: great things in business are never done by one person, they're done by a team of people."

—*Steve Jobs*

Picture this: the visionary who would one day reinvent the phone, the computer, even how we listen to music, suddenly powerless in the company he built.

In 1985, Steve Jobs wasn't just sidelined. He was outplayed in a corporate chess match through a boardroom coup that left him on the outside and defeated.

Imagine the tension in that room.

John Scully, the very CEO Jobs had recruited, standing before Apple's board with calm resolve. Around the table, executives leaned in, some nodding, some hesitant, as Scully painted Jobs as unfit to lead, rallying support behind his steadier style. Jobs, the dreamer, the disruptor, was effectively silenced in the empire he had created.

What Jobs needed in that moment wasn't another invention. He needed conviction that could inspire. He needed a remarkable moment; a message powerful enough to reclaim the room, to unite the board behind his vision, and to turn doubt into belief.

The kind of message that an inspiring coach delivers at halftime, when the team is battered and behind, but one fiery message convinces them the game isn't over, that victory is still possible.

That message never came.

History is full of moments when everything hinged on the right message.

Think of JFK's bold call to action: "Ask not what your country can do for you, ask what you can do for your country." Or Martin Luther King Jr.'s dream for equality, made deeply personal when he declared: "that my four little children will one day live in a nation where they will not be judged by the color of their skin but by the content of their character."

That's the level of remarkable communication Jobs needed in that boardroom. But Jobs was a tech genius, not yet a gifted orator. He was an innovator, not a communicator. He was an inventor, not yet a listener.

You may find it bold to reference JFK and MLK here but consider this: the impact of Jobs and Apple on civilization is undeniable. If he had resolved his differences with Scully and the board in 1985 and delivered a speech that truly captured the potential of Apple, could we have been holding the first iPhone in our hands any sooner? Would we have advanced more rapidly, with Jobs at the helm for more productive years? Or did his time away allow him to refine his vision, making possible the groundbreaking innovations we now take for granted?

Jobs' team turned on him in 1985.

His leadership style and communication skills weren't developed or refined enough to lead a team that perhaps wasn't yet remarkable? Reports from that time describe Jobs as volatile, intense, perfectionistic, and confrontational; traits often associated with genius. He had big ideas that needed to be shared, but like a tortured artist, he struggled to communicate them in a way that resonated with his team.

His vision was clear to him, but not to those around him. And because he wasn't listening, his team turned against him.

By 1997, when Jobs returned, Apple was on the brink of collapse. Reflecting on what had gone wrong, Jobs famously said that the company had "drifted away from doing the basics really well." Perhaps by then, Jobs had become the leader Apple truly needed, but he didn't just drift there.

His return wasn't merely a corporate wake-up call; it is a powerful reminder of how easily even the most innovative teams can lose sight of what truly matters. What Jobs couldn't communicate in 1985, saved Apple in 1997, when he could.

Remarkable teams understand that at the heart of every groundbreaking success (or failure) is the clarity and communication of their message.

This brings us to the second signature that marks a remarkable team: message.

> ## Key Signature #2
>
> Message: A compelling and consistent way of communicating what matters most, because everything communicates.

Everything Communicates

Functional teams often treat communication as a box to check: sending an email, delivering a speech, or putting out a memo. They assume that once words are spoken, the message has landed. As they communicate, functional teams often relegate their "message" to marketing managers, communications directors, or whatever department "owns" it—because it's their job.

Remarkable teams reach for something better. They know that everything communicates something.

Words, visuals, tone, and behavior all tell a story about who they are and what they value. And when those messages aren't aligned, the consequences can be costly.

Message underpins everything we do because every action, word, or even silence communicates something to those around us.

I remember a specific team I worked with where the leader spent time with me individually talking about how amazing his team was and how grateful he was to be surrounded by such talented leaders, but also expressing his frustration around the lid to progress they kept hitting.

I quickly confirmed my hunch when sitting through my following meetings with his key people that how he felt about them and the message he thought he was communicating was not being received or at best was being misinterpreted. For some they were feeling the exact opposite of what he hoped and it was absolutely creating the lid and affecting outcomes.

In 1985, Steve Jobs' leadership was sending an unhelpful, misaligned message—not just with his words, but with his actions, decisions, posture, and presence.

Research by UCLA Professor of Psychology Dr. Albert Mehrabian shows that nonverbal cues, tone, gestures, and actions, account for 93% of perceived communication.[4] Extend this concept to your team and the subconscious rhythms, actions, and assumptions that drive decisions, and you begin to see why message is such a vital focus for those reaching for remarkable.

---

[4] Eastman, Blake. "How Much of Communication Is Really Nonverbal? An Extensive Breakdown." *Nonverbal Group*, https://www.nonverbalgroup.com/general/how-much-of-communication-is-really-nonverbal-an-extensive-breakdow.

Better Messaging Requires Better Listening

Think of your favorite band, or perhaps you enjoy jazz or the symphony. These world-class examples display a perfect focus on message. Every instrument, every note contributes to the overall message of the music. The way each musician tunes their instrument, their energy levels, attitudes, and even their moments of silence (what and when they do and don't play) all enhance the performance and the message of the music. Like in music where discord, lack of harmony, or being out of tune or rhythm leads to a poor performance, misalignment between actions and words undercuts the message and erodes trust, which ultimately creates an underperforming team.

This is why remarkable teams treat message the same way the best musicians treat sound. Better messaging requires better listening.

One of the greatest lessons I learned as a musician was that communication isn't just about what you play. It's about what you hear. Young or less experienced musicians often want to show off, playing perfectly but without feeling or nuance. The greatest musicians, however, listen to what others are doing, complementing each other to create a cohesive, beautiful sound. In jazz, rock, or pop, the magic happens when musicians listen, complement, and improvise.

I remember sitting at the Blue Note Cafe in New York City with my youngest son, watching the Ron Carter Quartet,

Miles Davis's former bassist, perform. I was moved by how four musicians were so perfectly in sync, their energy and timing creating one cohesive, remarkable musical experience.

Remarkable teams understand that good listening is the bedrock for effective messaging. It's the foundation for understanding and alignment, both within teams and with external stakeholders.

According to a recent Gallup study, teams with leaders who actively listen show 32% higher engagement levels.[5] This is a clear indicator that listening leads to aligned messaging and higher performance. Remarkable teams actively listen to feedback, both intended and unintended, observe behaviors, and monitor the impact of their decisions, actions, and communication in real time. They remain attuned to others and approach daily interactions and long-term strategy with curiosity and openness to learn.

Remarkable teams understand that communication is a two-way street: they listen as much as they talk, seeking feedback to ensure clarity and alignment. That's why, when we add new team members, one of the first things we notice is how well they ask insightful questions and listen to the answers. Active listening isn't a side skill; it's the foundation of trust and alignment on any team.

---

[5] Harter, Jim. "Anemic Employee Engagement Points to Leadership Challenges." *Gallup Workplace*, 5 Aug. 2025.

While (as stated) communication is just as much about listening as it is about words it's also dangerous to assume people understand. You need to remember, it's not about what you said, it's about what others heard.

If you've ever said one thing and people did or reacted to another then you know what I'm talking about. If you're married, then you know!

It's happened to me many times in a team setting (although some may claim it was a disconnect with my Aussie accent).

A study by the International Listening Association reveals that most individuals retain only 25% of what they hear, even immediately after a conversation. This highlights the gap between what is communicated and what is actually understood.[6]

In team settings, unclear instructions from leaders often leads to a "failure to launch" or execute. For instance, a project leader might state a vision for success, but without confirming understanding, team members might interpret it differently.

Don't assume people understand, confirm it, because you can't communicate a remarkable message without being a remarkable listener.

---

[6] Vorecol Editorial Team. "What Role Does Active Listening Play in Effective Communication Skills Development?" *Vorecol Blog*, 28 Aug. 2024.

Message Traps

Effective communication is the cornerstone of a successful team, but too often, leaders and teams fall into the trap of assuming that their message is understood. Assumption traps us when we believe that what we're communicating is clear, that others care about the message, or that people automatically grasp our meaning. These assumptions can lead to misalignment, confusion, and a breakdown in trust. The challenge is that assumptions happen unconsciously, which is why we must work intentionally to recognize and overcome them.

This occurs when teams or leaders assume their message is clear or assume that others care and understand what's being communicated. This leads to misunderstanding and a failure to align with the audience. Assumptions fail to account for differences in perspective, experience, and understanding, and they can breed a dangerous false sense of clarity.

Without actively listening and verifying the impact of the message, assumptions run rampant. This leads to missed connections, lost opportunities, and sometimes even outright failure.

The Assuming Clarity Trap

Leaders think the message is obvious, but people hear different versions.

You share the plan in a meeting and heads nod around the table. You walk out confident that everyone is aligned. A week later, three teams have moved in three different directions. It feels like resistance. It is not. It is three honest interpretations of one message that was clear in your mind and fuzzy everywhere else.

Clarity does not come from volume, slide decks, or long memos. It comes from a single point stated in plain words, repeated until it may sound boring to you but clear to them. Complexity often masquerades as thoughtfulness, but in practice it produces drift. People fill in gaps with their own experience, their own language, and their own purpose. That is how a simple initiative divides into parallel efforts that veer off course.

Think about the way Apple narrowed focus during key seasons. The aim was not only better products. It was a cleaner message. One idea, expressed with precision, turned retail into a service experience. The store script sounded like normal conversation because the message behind it was consistent. The customer did not need a manual to understand it.

Leaders can build this kind of clarity in the room. State the outcome in one sentence that a new hire could explain at lunch. Ask for playback in the moment. Let someone else put your words into theirs. This is where two simple questions become powerful tools:

- Is what I am communicating clear?
- What is your understanding of this?

These questions reveal gaps that nods and silence often hide, allowing leaders to correct drift before it spreads.

If what comes back is different from what you intended, then restating and reworking in the moment buys you cheap clarity now instead of paying for expensive rework later. Clarity work can feel slow at first. But trust me, it's always faster than fixing confusion down the road.

Remarkable teams counter this trap by keeping messages simple and repeatable, restating the why behind the work until alignment becomes instinctive rather than assumed.

The Assuming Care Trap

Attention is presumed rather than earned through relevance and feedback.

We assume the team cares because we care. We are too close to the work. We know why it matters. Others are juggling full plates and competing goals. They do not owe us their attention. We must earn it. Simone Weil called attention the "rarest and purest form of generosity."[7] Treat it like a gift and people will give you more.

Earning attention begins with relevance. Start where their world hurts or hopes. Name the stakes in concrete terms.

---

[7] Toh, Justine. "Your Attention Is the Rarest and Purest Form of Generosity." *Seen & Unseen*, 17 Nov. 2023.

Invite them into the story early. Then prove that their voice changes the outcome. When Starbucks opened a door for customer input and acted on what it heard, people did not just feel informed. They felt included. Free WIFI and mobile ordering were not slogans. They were visible responses to real feedback.

Attention is also a rhythm. You cannot surge once and then coast. The modern workplace is loud. A message competes with chats, emails, and notifications. Good leaders communicate openly, often and with strength, they connect to what people value, and circle back to show what changed because people spoke up. That loop builds trust. Over time the audience learns that speaking, listening and seeking to understand is worth the effort.

You can feel the difference when care is present. Meetings lift. Energy rises. People ask better questions and volunteer to own pieces of the work. You can also feel the absence. Faces are blank. Notes are thin. Follow through is late or off target. That is not a character flaw. It is a signal that the message did not become meaningful. Go back. Make it matter to them, not just to you.

Remarkable teams avoid the Assuming Care Trap by earning attention on purpose, tying every message back to mission and to the real lives of the people receiving it.

The Assuming Understanding Trap

When there is no confirmation of what was received, action stalls or goes sideways.

Nods do not equal understanding. Neither do smiles or silence. Real understanding shows up as aligned action. When teams leave a room with different pictures in their minds, they work hard and still there is a disconnect. That is demoralizing. It is also avoidable.

The simplest way to prevent it is to verify in the moment. Ask what people are taking away. Ask what will happen first and who will do it. Write down the exact words you all agree on and put them where everyone can see. This is not a test. It is a kindness. It saves people from doing the wrong thing right. It saves you from discovering three weeks later that the train left the station on the wrong track.

Remember that words are not the only signals. Hiring choices, how you recognize people, how you run reviews, and how you spend budget all broadcast meaning. If your stated message and your visible choices do not line up, the choices will win. People will believe what you do over what you say. Close that gap and understanding will result.

There is courage in asking, "What is your understanding of this? There is also humility in hearing the answer and adjusting your message. When you do, work speeds up. Productivity becomes aligned and effective. People own their part with confidence because they know exactly what success looks like and when it's due. That is how shared understanding turns into shared momentum.

When you defeat these three assumptions, communication stops being an announcement and becomes a shared effort. Say it simply until it is familiar and repeatable. Earn attention by making it matter and by acting on what you hear. Confirm understanding before the work begins.

Remarkable teams defeat the Assuming Understanding Trap by validating understanding before work begins, creating a rhythm of playback, clarity checks, and visible agreements.

Message Priorities

Remarkable teams understand that communication is a two-way street: they listen as much as they talk. They actively seek feedback to ensure clarity and alignment. This approach to communication is foundational when building trust and reaching for remarkable.

Effective communication becomes a powerful tool when it's used intentionally. It optimizes messages and transforms impact. But none of this happens by accident, it takes systems and discipline to make communication intentional.

My friend and communications expert Phil Bowdle says: "Communication isn't somebody's job. It's everybody's job, and you have a role to play." This mentality is essential because everything, at every level of the organization, rises and falls on clear communication. That's why building systems for intentional communication is so important. These systems will be unique to your team and organization.

As you design initiatives to keep your communication on track, here are the key priorities to drive those conversations.

Priority #1—Grow a Listening Culture

Encourage curiosity and openness through team norms and leadership modeling. For our team, "Be Curious" is a mantra that automatically elevates listening. I've written before about my own inclination toward asking questions, and I encourage teams to adopt this value as it strengthens the core of intentional communication.

Regularly practice reflective listening exercises to sharpen active listening skills. These practices can become second nature and will help clarify communication with simple phrases like:

- "Can you clarify what you just heard?"
- "Tell me more."
- "Here's what I heard. Can you confirm or add clarity?"

As a leader, model this behavior consistently. Train and retrain your team on the importance of active listening and creating spaces for collaboration and feedback.

Priority #2—Develop Feedback Loops

Creating mechanisms for gathering and responding to feedback is crucial. We've seen this in action with organizations like charity: water, which uses feedback loops to remain transparent and accountable. It's also rare that I land at my home airport in Denver without immediately receiving an email asking for feedback from United Airlines. Similarly, my boots are barely off after a day skiing before a text arrives that asks about my experience (and yes the lift lines are always too long). This level of attention to feedback, whether from customers, partners, or team members, is vital for intentional communication.

Feedback loops are essential in any setting, especially in faith-based and nonprofit organizations, where transparency with constituents and members is key. At Slingshot, we've used surveys to gather valuable feedback, but nothing compares to relational follow-ups that dig deeper into what can be improved.

Just as important is internal team feedback. We survey our team annually, and this is equally vital to how we increase effectiveness.

An example from Toyota illustrates the power of real-time feedback: their "Andon Cord," can be pulled by any worker on the production line to immediately stop the line if they detect a problem. This allows immediate response, helping ensure quality and alignment with company standards.

Does your team have permission to pull the "Andon Cord?"

Priority #3—Clarify the Message

Ensure alignment between what's communicated and how it's perceived.

By doing clarity checks at every level of the organization, you avoid the pitfalls of people simply performing tasks without understanding their purpose. This is where alignment with the greater mission matters. Consider Toyota's example again. Workers on the production line don't just do their jobs; they understand how their work contributes to Toyota's mission of "Producing Happiness for All" and "Creating Mobility for All."

Clarifying the message at every level promotes a sense of conviction and helps move teams toward remarkable outcomes.

Priority #4—Adapt Communication Styles

Tailor communication methods to different situations and audiences. Communication is not a one-size-fits-all approach. Whether you're addressing a team, presenting to partners, updating customers, or communicating with volunteers, adjusting your style is crucial.

When we work with new organizations, we always ask about their "preferred mode of communication," whether it's email, text, phone calls, or team communication platform tools. Understanding these preferences ensures that our communication is efficient and effective.

Sometimes, communication styles need to adapt in response to an event or crisis. For example, Airbnb shifted its messaging to resonate with hosts and travelers during the COVID-19 pandemic, demonstrating the adaptability needed when dealing with the unexpected or even unimagined.

I resonated with a LinkedIn[8] article on adapting communication style that suggested five essential steps:

1. Assess the situation.
2. Respect differences.
3. Adapt your style.
4. Seek feedback.
5. Be flexible.

The adaptability of your communication will determine how effectively your message is received.

Priority #5—Close the Loop

The final step in building systems for intentional communication and clarity of message is to close the loop on feedback. Remember: people don't do what you expect—they do what you inspect. So, show that you are listening by following up on feedback, checking in on (and monitoring) progress and celebrating clarity and change.

---

[8] "How Do You Adapt Your Communication Style?" LinkedIn, accessed March 4, 2026, https://www.linkedin.com/advice/0/how-do-you-adapt-your-communication-style-ucxwf.

Charity: water's commitment to reporting how feedback has shaped their initiatives is a great example of closing the loop and building donor trust. If feedback is received but not acted upon or monitored, the relationship weakens.

When we receive feedback through surveys or evaluations, we ensure that we follow up by outlining how we'll address the feedback, what actions we'll take, and how we'll report back on progress. This process includes:

1. Documenting feedback.
2. Setting objectives based on the feedback.
3. Creating a follow-up schedule.
4. Following through as promised.

Closing the loop is a key way to deepen trust and brand loyalty. Don't miss the opportunity to demonstrate that you're actively responding and improving.

The Power of Intentional Communication: Key Results and Impact

The systems and priorities around intentional communication are vital to leveraging the full power and impact of our second key signature. When done well, the results can be transformative, leading teams down the path to remarkable outcomes. Here's how intentional communication drives success:

Deepening Trust and Alignment

Consistent and intentional messaging builds trust within teams and with external stakeholders. This deepened trust accelerates team performance by reducing unhealthy friction caused by suspicion, confusion, and dissatisfaction. Stephen Covey's *The Speed of Trust* outlines actionable strategies for leaders to build trust and alignment, helping teams achieve remarkable results more quickly. He describes what he calls a "trust tax," there is an invisible toll of low trust resulting in things like extra meetings, delays, rework, second guessing, approvals and turnover. The more trust improves, the lower the tax, the tighter the alignment and the faster the work flows with fewer detours.[9]

Organizational alignment to a remarkable team is the oil that helps the cogs and pistons move smoothly in an engine.

Amplifying Team Influence

Intentional communication refines and clarifies the team's vision, transforming a collective message that resonates deeply with others. SpaceX's clear, bold mission to "make life multiplanetary" is a perfect example. This vision not only inspires employees but also creates advocates among partners and the public, amplifying their message far beyond the company itself.

---

[9] Covey, Stephen M. R., with Rebecca R. Merrill. *The Speed of Trust: The One Thing That Changes Everything*. Free Press, 2006, p.250.

Driving Innovation

Clear, intentional communication at every level of an organization sets the stage for innovation. When team members feel heard and valued, they're more likely to share ideas that push the mission forward. Innovation thrives when the culture supports open communication, as people feel safe to express new thoughts and solutions. Some of the most significant innovations have been born out of a culture of openness and clear, intentional communication and you wouldn't believe how many amazing things have happened and been invented by accident because of an intentionally trusting and collaborative environment.

Strengthening Organizational Resilience

Listening and adaptive communication are crucial when navigating challenges. Even the most remarkable teams don't get everything right all the time. But what sets them apart is how they respond when things go wrong. Intentional communication equips teams to respond constructively, course-correcting when necessary to maintain focus and drive.

A prime example is Netflix's ability to pivot its business model from DVDs to streaming, then into original content. In *No Rules Rules*, Reed Hastings and Erin Meyer delve into how Netflix's culture of open feedback and adaptive communication allowed them to thrive in a constantly evolving market. Their growth and market leadership are a testament to the power of intentional, adaptive communication.[10]

Remember the overarching theme here for the key signature of Message: Everything Communicates! Every word, every action, and every behavior sends a message, shaping your team's culture and impact.

Daniel Coyle's *The Culture Code* further emphasizes this when he explains that everything a team does communicates something. He introduces the idea of "signals of safety," where intentional communication creates trust and openness, empowering team members to feel valued and heard. Leaders play a pivotal role in setting the tone for these signals. Even subtle cues can either strengthen or undermine team cohesion.[11] Coyle's examples, like Pixar and the Navy SEALs, show how shared vulnerability and active listening create environments where communication becomes a powerful tool for connection, alignment, and innovation.

Intentionality and alignment should be embedded into every aspect of communication. The practices Coyle describes, shared vulnerability, active listening, and feedback loops, help teams create trust-rich environments where individuals

---

[10] Hastings, Reed, and Erin Meyer. *No Rules Rules: Netflix and the Culture of Reinvention*. Penguin Press, 2020.

[11] Coyle, Daniel. *The Culture Code: The Secrets of Highly Successful Groups*. Bantam, 2018, 99.

feel empowered to speak openly, ask questions, offer feedback, and address misunderstandings. Leaders who model these behaviors set a consistent tone, aligning words with actions to reinforce clarity, purpose, and alignment.[12]

The journey to remarkable communication requires vigilance. As we outlined earlier, assumptions and unconscious bias can create barriers to effective communication. That's why it's essential to encourage open feedback loops within your team and establish a culture of trust where these things can be addressed.

We call this the "last 10%," asking "What aren't people saying?" Leaders must actively seek these unspoken truths to keep the lines of communication clear and free from misunderstanding.

A Call to Action

Prioritize listening and feedback as part of your ongoing commitment to intentional communication and healthy messaging. Conduct regular team reviews and communication audits to ensure your message remains aligned and clear. These practices will be foundational to your team's success on the path to remarkable.

Steve Jobs' journey is a prime example of how effective communication can lead to extraordinary results. In his

---

[12] Ibid, 24-25, 121-124, 115-117.

2005 Stanford Commencement Address he famously said, "You can't connect the dots looking forward; you can only connect them looking backward." Reflecting on his journey, he emphasized the vitality of message and intentional communication. He saw a reality without it in 1985 and what a difference it can make moving a mission forward post '97.

He went on to say, "Sometimes life hits you in the head with a brick. Don't lose faith." For our context here, this is a reminder not to let setbacks derail our commitment to intentional communication—even when things don't go as planned.

The greatest quote from Jobs' speech, "Remembering that you are going to die is the best way I know to avoid the trap of thinking you have something to lose."

Your leadership, your team, and your life communicate a message. You get to choose whether it's functional, remarkable, or just noise. Reach for a message that's remarkable, your mission needs it. Your mission deserves it.

CHAPTER 5
CULTURE

SIGNATURE #3 CULTURE

Values and behaviors that shape the soul of your team.

"The culture of one soul affects the culture of all souls."

—Ralph Waldo Emerson

Walking into this large organization I remember how the lobby buzzed with energy. Volunteers were greeting each other. The staff was smiling. The mission was posted everywhere on the walls—bold, clear, inspiring. If you had walked through with me, you'd have thought, "This place is alive. This culture is strong."

And when I sat down with the executive leaders, that's exactly what I heard.

Stories of unity. A staff driven by values like humility, accountability, integrity. A deep commitment to their mission.

But as the day unfolded, a different picture emerged. In smaller rooms, behind closed doors, I heard quieter voices. Staff members who hesitated before speaking. People who loved the mission but felt unseen. Patterns of behavior that didn't quite match the mission posted on the walls. Comments like, "We don't really say that out loud" or "It's just easier not to ask questions."

This organization, which I'm intentionally leaving unnamed out of respect for the people involved, would later walk through a very public season of pain. Leaders stepped down. Trust was shaken. And the heartbreaking part was that the mission never changed. The mission was still compelling. The values were still noble. The intentions were sincere.

What fractured was the alignment between those values and the behaviors.

I've seen this pattern across countless teams. The values and mission aren't the issue. The problem is the gap between what a team says it is . . . and how people actually experience it.

Leaders describe the culture they believe they're building. Team members describe the culture they're actually living in. And when those two stories drift apart, the soul of the organization starts to split.

Because ultimately, a team's culture isn't defined by its statements. It's defined by its behaviors.

When values and behavior align, the culture of a team can become a powerful force to carry a remarkable mission forward. When they don't, even the most remarkable mission isn't enough.

> ## Key Signature #3
> Culture: Values and behaviors that shape the soul of your team.

Culture as the Soul of a Team

Ralph Waldo Emerson once said that culture reveals the soul not just of an organization, but of humanity itself.

Culture is the unseen force that shapes teams, much like the soul shapes individuals and collective souls shape a country. Similar to the last chapter that everything communicates a message, your team's culture is being shaped by every interaction and every moment.

A team's culture is its heart. If the culture is unhealthy, the team can quickly become toxic, damaging, ineffective, and memorable (even newsworthy) for all the wrong reasons. But when the culture is healthy, anything becomes possible.

The health of the team's soul, or as we more commonly call it, the culture, depends on two key forces working together: behavior and relationships.

Behavior Shaping Culture

Every team has values that they want to live out as part of their culture. They're written into handbooks, framed in hallways, shared in onboarding decks, and repeated in staff meetings. And most of the time, they're inspiring.

I've never worked with a team whose stated values were the problem. In fact, if value statements alone could build a remarkable culture, most teams would already have one. But values on a wall don't shape culture, behaviors do.

Over the years, we have talked with countless leaders who were looking for new opportunities because of unhealthy culture. Often, these candidates were drawn to a role because of a team's mission and stated values. On paper, everything lined up. In the interview process, everything looked healthy. But once they arrived, the day-to-day behaviors told a different story. The mission was inspiring, but the culture they lived wasn't the culture they were promised. And now, they're needing to exit to find a better culture fit.

What leaders tolerate, model, and reinforce, in the everyday moments, is what actually forms the soul of a team.

If we say that we value honesty but avoid hard conversations, then honesty never becomes normal practice and our culture drifts away from becoming remarkable.

If we say that we value unity but shut down differing opinions, then unity becomes uniformity and our culture loses the healthy tension required for remarkable teamwork.

If we say that we value excellence but reward speed over quality, then excellence turns into exhaustion and our culture cannot grow into something remarkable.

Remarkable teams pay as much attention to the behaviors surrounding those values as the values themselves. They understand that a value like "honesty" requires behaviors like timely feedback. A value like "unity" requires behaviors like healthy disagreement. A value like "humility" requires behaviors like sharing credit and owning mistakes.

Values name the aspiration. Behaviors determine whether that aspiration becomes reality.

The organization in the opening story is a vivid example. Their values were solid. Their mission was powerful. Their intentions were sincere. But the behaviors inside the team—the hesitations, the silence, the unspoken rules—told a different cultural story.

But behavior alone doesn't tell the whole story of culture. How those behaviors land—and how deeply they take root—depends on the strength of the relationships within the team.

Relationships Shaping Culture

In our work over the last two decades, we've found that the number one cause of breakdown in team relationships and leadership health is a lack of relational equity.

Relational equity is the trust, goodwill, and emotional capital built over time within a team. It's like a "relationship bank account" where positive interactions are deposits, and conflicts or neglect are withdrawals.

Relationships have always been my starting point, which is why this key signature resonates so deeply for me. I have long been fascinated by how people connect, and I have come to believe that strong relationships are the foundation of a healthy culture.

I remember my first leadership role. I was young and had just moved from Hobart, Tasmania to Sydney, NSW for a Music Director position. A mentor who was familiar with the relational landscape gave me a pre-brief on my biggest relational challenge. This individual, much older than me and a prominent member of the leadership board, had a strong sense of ownership over the area I would be leading. I look back now and see that moment as a challenge—a gauntlet thrown down. Instead of avoiding this relationship, I embraced it.

We met regularly. I approached the relationship with a mindset of learning and curiosity, investing in relational equity. Over time, I grew to appreciate his story and motivations. When changes were made that weren't his "preference," I had enough relational equity to explain the "purpose" behind those changes and earn his support. As a result, the mission moved forward.

When it came time for me to leave that organization and move to the United States, he made a speech at my farewell that reflected how much relational equity we had built together.

Years later, I encountered a similar challenge in a new organization in a different country and culture. Once again, I faced an individual with a sense of ownership over the area I was leading, who was much older than me and held a prominent position. Another gauntlet was thrown, and another deep and treasured friendship formed.

This time, when I took part in his funeral years later, I was able to express my appreciation for his investment in me. I believe our relationship had matured from a "relationship bank account" into something truly meaningful. Both of these individuals played a significant role in supporting the soul health (culture) of our team.

Remarkable culture starts with relationships and grows when we continue to pay attention to relationships. So many leaders forget this and wonder why team culture remains functional at best or turns toxic at worst.

From 2012 to 2015, Google conducted an extensive study called Project Aristotle, aiming to identify the key factors behind high-performing teams. They found that the most critical factor for team performance was psychological safety, team members' belief that they can take risks and be vulnerable without fear of judgment. Their research pointed to psychological safety being rooted in strong interpersonal relationships and trust.[13]

While performance metrics are absolutely necessary, teams that prioritize open communication, mutual respect, and a sense of belonging are aiming for something truly remarkable.

Teams with strong relational equity show resilience during challenges, greater collaboration, and improved problem-solving.

To use our earlier flight analogy: relational investments made at 30,000 feet give context to decisions and challenges at 10,000 feet or when you land on the ground. Or, more simply put, you do not want to be writing checks from your relational bank account that you cannot cash.

---

[13] Duhigg, Charles. "What Google Learned From Its Quest to Build the Perfect Team." *The New York Times Magazine*, 25 Feb. 2016.

I have worked with and coached teams where you can trace their success back to consistent relational habits and investments. These teams have sustained success and high levels of output.

Trust, loyalty, longevity, and a willingness to go above and beyond the call of duty point to a team culture where members feel cared for beyond what they can produce. As a result, they often produce even more.

I can think of organizations where, even before meeting the team leader, you can feel their influence. When you meet them, you can see how they have hired and developed people to exponentially grow relational investment throughout the team.

What I have never seen is this happening by accident. It is always intentional.

Leaders of remarkable teams know where to prioritize relational investment, because it yields compound interest and exponential impact. They realize the importance of this key signature.

Notable examples of organizations that do this well include:

- **Southwest Airlines:** Their commitment to exceptional customer service flows from how they treat their own team members. Staff who feel appreciated and loyal translate that loyalty into profitability and brand strength in a competitive market.

- **Starbucks:** Known for referring to its employees as "partners," Starbucks invests in generous benefits and equity in decision-making. This communicates deep care for their staff.

- **Microsoft:** Under the leadership of Satya Nadella, Microsoft developed a culture of empathy, collaboration, inclusion, and empowerment. This culture translated into accelerated growth in cloud computing and AI development.

- **Habitat for Humanity:** This nonprofit's model is based on relational equity. Their team members work closely alongside the homeowners they serve, building relationships that contribute to the organization's continued global impact.

However, in any organization, there is a trap of becoming so focused on caring for the people being served that we neglect relational investment in those we serve with—our own team.

This often starts at the board level, where members, volunteering their time, may not prioritize relational investment with one another. Without relational equity, poor communication, lack of trust, and inadequate collaboration can create dysfunction, compromising an organization's effectiveness.

We cannot underestimate the importance of intentional investment in relational equity. Without it, teams risk missing the opportunity to overcome challenges and fulfill their missions.

Culture Traps

Many teams assume they are investing relationally when, in reality, they are barely scratching the surface. Quick greetings, polite hallway chats, or a casual message can feel friendly, but they do not build the trust that advancing a mission requires. When leaders focus on progress and tasks while overlooking emotional and relational needs, momentum slows. People hesitate to fully invest. Culture grows thin.

This is why remarkable teams pay attention not just to what builds relational health but also to what undermines it. After years of coaching leaders, building, and working with teams, three relational traps show up again and again. They look harmless on the surface, but each one quietly erodes trust, weakens culture, and limits mission impact. Understanding these traps is the first step to avoiding them.

Here are the three traps to watch for.

The Shallow Trap

Quick check-ins replace real care, so trust never takes root.

Superficial exchanges like, "Hey, how's it going?" Or a quick digital check in are not enough. They lack the substance needed to build lasting trust and a true bond. True relational equity grows through consistent, intentional actions. It shows up in real conversations, honest celebration, and steady presence.

Leaders often believe relationships are stronger than they are. The result is a slow fade of cohesion and care. Teams do not feel seen. They disconnect from the mission. The culture becomes fragile.

To stay healthy, go beyond polite touch points. Build a regular rhythm of personal check-ins that feel human. Ask how people are doing. Listen without rushing to fix. Celebrate the quiet wins that no one sees. As Marcus Buckingham said, "People don't need feedback; they need attention (to what they do best)."[14] Active listening and curiosity signal value. They also open the door to belonging.

Healthy teams measure the health of their relationships. Use regular reviews that ask about care, value, and emotional safety. Add an annual survey that looks at relational, team, and cultural health. This feedback loop reveals early signs of neglect. You can then course correct before small issues grow large.

Culture is what you do. Not just what you say. If your values claim inclusion, live that out in hiring. Make space for every voice. When words and actions do not match, people read a lack of care. Trust slips. Engagement drops.

Care includes how you end roles. Ending a role is hard. Do it with dignity and clarity. If a departure (based on

---

[14] Buckingham, Marcus, and Ashley Goodall. "The Feedback Fallacy." *Harvard Business Review*, Mar.–Apr. 2019.

performance) surprises the team member or the team, then performance conversations were not happening. Coach up or coach out with attention and care. Respectful endings protect culture. They communicate that people matter, even in hard moments.

Relational deposits work like vitamins. They only help when taken over time. Stop investing and culture weakens. Toxic behaviors creep in. Coaching sessions and team health assessments surface the same pain point statements like:

"I do not feel valued for what I uniquely bring."

"I rarely connect socially with my team leader."

"I wish I felt more connected to the team."

"I do not feel like my voice is heard."

These statements trace back to thin deposits and low trust.

Research echoes the pattern. Leaders often shift attention from relational priorities to urgent tasks and easy metrics. McKinsey reports that only 52 percent of executives feel their time aligns with strategic priorities. Relational investment gets overlooked.

Results suffer.[15]

---

[15] Bevins, Frankki, and Aaron De Smet. "Making Time Management the Organization's Priority." *McKinsey Quarterly*, 2013.

The Avoidance Trap

Hard conversations are delayed, which erodes safety and teamwork.

Conflict is natural. It is also necessary. Teams that avoid it weaken culture. Avoidance shuts down learning, blocks resolution, and undermines trust. A false peace settles in while tensions simmer. Over time, collaboration erodes.

Leaders who address conflict with empathy build safety and commitment. Constructive conflict can strengthen a team. It creates shared understanding. It restores trust. It clears the air so people can create together again.

Avoiding hard conversations is not care. It is neglect. It denies the team a chance to grow. Healthy teams name the issue, listen well, and pursue repair. They treat conflict as a chance to practice their values in real time.

Remember that culture is how your team experiences your organization. In 2002, I moved to the United States. I learned quickly how distinct and different a country's culture can be. The learning curve was huge in so many ways. We were experiencing in real time a new culture we had only imagined and seen in movies and on TV. Add to that the challenge that people often stopped listening to our words and focused more on how we said them. It was trusted relationships with new friends who listened to our challenges that helped us adjust. We did the same for our friend Kate as she encountered the same learning curve

when she arrived. Australia is obviously a different culture
from the U.S!

McDonalds is different from Chick-fil-A.
Walmart is different from Target.
World Vision is different from Compassion International.
Your church is different from the one down the street.
(That's why there are so many.) Culture is distinct.
Differences create ripple effects. Healthy uniqueness should
be celebrated. It also must be stewarded in conflict. If we
were all the same, we would be boring and forgettable. Real
conversations help differences work together.

The Transactional Trap

Connections stay task only, so belonging and commitment
stay thin.

In this Trap, relationships remain functional. Members
move tasks across the board but do not build bonds. Work
gets done in the short term. Engagement and loyalty fade in
the long term.

Functional exchanges are necessary. They are not sufficient.
Teams need space to express emotion and be heard. Leaders
who invest in relational equity create those spaces. They
go beyond status updates. They ask better questions. They
make time for stories. They invite people to share what is
working and what is heavy. They notice and name the good.

When leaders prioritize these deeper practices, people feel valued as people. Not only as workers. Belonging increases. Commitment deepens. The mission grows because the team has roots.

To keep relationships from staying thin, build simple habits. Schedule regular personal check-ins. Include a few cultural health questions in team reviews. Model vulnerability and openness. Follow through on what you say. Show how decisions reflect stated values. These behaviors move a team from transactions to trust.

Teams that invest in relational equity thrive. There are no quick fixes. Deposits only grow over time. When leaders address relational needs, step into discomfort, and build a culture of trust, there is greater productivity and healthier engagement and transformative collaboration. People stay connected to the mission through storms and change.

This all underscores a simple truth. Culture is how you behave. It is how your team and those you serve experience your organization. Lead with steady care. Have hard conversations with empathy. Build connections that go beyond tasks. Do this, and the story of your team will carry real weight, one relationship at a time.

Culture Priorities

At the risk of restating but to break it down into intentional practices to build a winning, healthy culture on the pathway to remarkable, here are things you should be doing regularly:

- **One-on-One Check-Ins:** Scheduling consistent individual meetings allows leaders to give attention to their team members and understand their concerns, provide personalized feedback, and build trust. These interactions create a platform for open communication and strengthen relationships.

- **Celebrate Team Successes:** Acknowledging and celebrating achievements boost morale and reinforce a sense of belonging. Recognizing both individual and collective accomplishments creates a positive team environment.

- **Provide Consistent Feedback:** Offering regular, constructive feedback helps team members grow and feel valued. It encourages continuous improvement and demonstrates a leader's commitment to their team's development.

- **Continuous Care Initiatives:** Scheduling connection time with key team members who will also extend and uphold this culture of care to others in the organization. This helps deepen relational equity and reinforces (and reproduces) the emotional connection within the team.

- **Mentorship Moments:** Creating intentional opportunities for experienced team members to pour into others promotes growth, confidence, and shared wisdom. These relationships accelerate development and reinforce a culture where people invest in one another.

- **Team Retreats or Reset Days:** Stepping away from the normal rhythm gives a team space to reconnect, reflect, and refocus. Whether it's a half-day offsite or a multi-day retreat, these moments strengthen trust, deepen relationships, and renew shared purpose.

- **Meaningful Rhythms and Rituals:** Building simple, repeatable practices into the life of your team reinforces identity and belonging. This could be a weekly story of impact, a shared meal, a moment of prayer, or a tradition unique to your team. Consistent rhythms create connection and anchor culture in ways words alone never can.

This all builds the invaluable intangible but powerful trust that is always evident in remarkable teams. Patrick Lencioni emphasizes that trust is the foundation of a successful team, enabling open communication and effective collaboration. I would add that it's also the foundation of the healthy soul of your team.

In Joseph Folkman's book The Trifecta of Trust, he claims that employees in high-trust environments report:

- 40% less burnout
- 66% more closeness with colleagues
- 50% higher productivity
- 13% fewer sick days
- 106% more energy at work
- 70% more alignment with the company's purpose
- 17% higher compensation than their peers in low-trust companies
- 29% more satisfaction with their lives[16]

Trust is the foundation for healthy culture which translates to healthy leaders which translates to a healthy team. The results are not just compelling they help you reach for remarkable!

At the risk of stating the obvious about culture, you can't fake it; you must live it. Again, it's about what you do and how you behave that shapes the soul of your team. It's the sum of who you are and how you're experienced. Just like soul music was an extension of the experienced oppression of a people group, your team's soul is an extension of your team's experience.

---

[16] Folkman, Joseph R. The Trifecta of Trust: The Proven Formula for Gaining and Maintaining Trust as a Leader. Zenger Folkman Press, 2022, pp. 24–26.

Remarkable culture will always win, and at its core, it's about people.

What do I love about the new culture I adopted when we moved from Australia to the USA years ago? People!

What do I miss about the country we left behind? People.

What are the trophies in the trophy cabinet of my heart from the different teams I've been a part of and led over the years? They all have to do with people.

People make up your culture, so you'd better start prioritizing attention to them. Results only follow investment in people.

I also believe that authentic love is found in the soil of remarkable teams. Apologies if this chapter and key signature is ending a little "touchy-feely."

Tim Sanders in his book Love Is The Killer App wrote:

> *"The most powerful force in business isn't greed, fear, or even the raw energy of unbridled competition. The most powerful force in business is love. It's what will help your company grow and become stronger. It's what will propel your career forward. It's what will give you a sense of meaning and satisfaction in your work, which will help you do your best work."*[17]

---

[17] Sanders, Tim. "Love Is the Killer App." *Fast Company*, 31 Jan. 2002.

Love is such a subjective word. It carries all kinds of emotional weight, and differing definitions for each of us, shaped most profoundly by our unique experiences.

Sanders goes on to quote Milton Mayeroff with this definition of love: "Love, he writes, is the selfless promotion of the growth of the other. When you help others grow to become the best people that they can be, you are being loving, and as a result, you grow."[18]

Sounds like remarkable culture! Your team not only needs it, it'll struggle, or at best, remain functional, without it.

---

[18] Sanders, Tim. *Love Is the Killer App: How to Win Business and Influence Friends.* Crown Business, 2002.

CHAPTER 6
ROLES

CHAPTER 6

SIGNATURE #4 ROLES

Unique contributions for remarkable impact

---

*"You don't build a business—you build people—
and then people build the business."*

—*Zig Ziglar*

Naturally drawn to and inspired by music, I vividly remember listening to '33s on a turntable in our living room and being captivated at an early age by the creativity of world-class jazz musicians as they communicated through the shared language of improvisation.

I felt the same wonder listening to a symphony orchestra come together to perform a structured masterpiece.

I felt that same spark years later when I encountered the bold, soaring sound of U2.

U2 is a rare example of lasting success, blending commercial longevity, critical acclaim, and global influence. Over more than four decades, they've sold over 170 million records, won 22 Grammy Awards, and were inducted into the Rock and Roll Hall of Fame in 2005.

Still, one has to wonder: What makes them unique?

U2 mastered a unique and genre-defining sound through an innovative approach that redefined musical genius by blending elements of post-punk, alternative rock, and atmospheric, delay heavy guitar work.

It was a team effort! And it all started with scenius.
What the heck is scenius?
I'm glad you asked . . .

This unique approach inspired producer Brian Eno, famous for his work with U2, Talking Heads, Devo, and Coldplay, to coin the term scenius. He said:

> *"Scenius is the intelligence of a whole operation or group of people. Let's forget the idea of 'genius' for a little while, let's think about the whole ecology of ideas that give rise to good new thoughts and good new work."*[19]

---

[19] "Luminous Sydney 2009 (Part 2)." *More Dark Than Shark*, transcribed by radiocitizen, 26 May 2009, https://www.moredark thanshark.org/feature_luminous2.html

The band's success was no accident. They intentionally cultivated a culture where every team member's voice mattered, musical risk was welcomed, and deep convictions along with creative friction led to a lasting worldwide impact for decades. It wasn't just the genius of Bono or any one individual in U2, it was "scenius" at work.

Brilliance that consistently emerges and reinvents itself from a group, rather than a single individual, is exceptionally rare in the creative space. They have relentlessly refined who they are, clarified each member's role, and continually elevated one another's contributions.

While U2's mark on the entertainment world is unique and unmatched, I would suggest that their shared set of values, if examined closely, aligns with many mission-aligned teams doing great work. It all points back to Eno's concept of scenius: the most notable results happen together, collectively.

A question has always intrigued me: would any of these iconic band members have been legendary on their own? Somehow, I doubt it.

> ## Key Signature #4
>
> ## Roles: Unique contributions for remarkable impact

What do you do when you step into a new role, a new city, or a new season and suddenly realize you cannot succeed on your own?

I arrived in Sydney from my hometown of Hobart in February 1993 with a head full of dreams, a handful of ideas, and the promise of a very part-time job as a church Music Director. I think my family expected I'd be back in Tasmania within weeks or months. Instead, that part-time job grew into a nine-year commitment to an organization with a compelling and growing mission, one that shaped my life and leadership in ways I couldn't have imagined as I simply put one foot in front of the other.

What I did know was that I couldn't build anything alone. I needed other people. So, I got busy developing relationships. In the process, I learned a lot about who I was and, more importantly, who I wasn't.

This requires one of the scariest qualities of team leadership—vulnerability. I learnt in those early days that gut level honesty about who I was, and what I wanted to do and achieve, while also having a sane understanding of my abilities, allowed me to engage in healthy authentic team relationships and to learn quickly from those around me. This open-handed approach leads to the most powerful yet terrifying statements in leadership:

I don't know.
I don't know what to do.
I don't know how to get there.
I don't know how to build this.
I don't know what the next best step is.

When we admit we don't know, our mission immediately becomes bigger than ourselves. We realize we need others to help us achieve it, and we have to determine what role each person will play in moving it forward.

By the end of those nine years, I had learned how to build and inspire volunteer teams, collaborate creatively with people who often exceeded me in skill, and grow exponentially through those partnerships. I gained self-awareness by working on a team that took personality profiles seriously. In my twenties, I came face-to-face with both my strengths and my glaring weaknesses. The fast-paced environment demanded I adjust quickly or risk not making it.

When an unexpected opportunity arose from an organization ten times the size and across the world, I was so committed to the work and community in Sydney that I almost missed what was clearly my next chapter. But as often happens when you look in the rearview mirror (some call it fate and others call it purpose or calling) the signs were unmistakable.

As plans for the move to the United States and a new role in Colorado began to take shape, I asked a trusted friend and colleague if he thought I was ready for this next level of leadership. His response crystallized our next key signature.

He said, "As long as you have the right people around you in the right roles."

Then he pointed out exactly what kind of support he thought I would need.

He was right. And I listened. Why? Because I had learned that if you want to serve a remarkable mission, you need a remarkable team.

A remarkable mission is always bigger than you and it has to be. You can't be the lid on the mission or the cap on your team. Many leaders end up unintentionally leading their teams to mediocrity and their missions to just a memory because they fail to recognize this.

Leaders who reach for remarkable know it starts with "team design"—people in the right roles; roles that complement, stretch, support, and bring out each other's best.

A remarkable team embraces the unique roles of its members as mission critical, ensuring clarity, trust, and aligned contribution across the team by activating each person's God-given gifts and responsibilities.

Beyond Unicorns

Every leader has been there—maybe you're there right now. You find yourself asking, *What's next? Who's next? How do we get unstuck?*

Questions like these often flow from the "I don't know" statements we explored earlier.

We've found that most organizational challenges trace back to a person:

- The need for someone new.
- The need for an existing team member to break through to the next level of leadership.
- The need for an idea or perspective that isn't currently in the room or around the table.

Which leads to even more powerful questions:

Do I add someone? Do I add someone who thinks like me? Do I add someone who will challenge me? What are the outcomes and wins if I do?

Friends, I'm not inventing a new mountain to climb here when it comes to roles on your team and the complexity of defining, staffing, and developing them. Perhaps I'm just a sherpa, helping you know where to place your next step as you climb.

Let's simplify.

Think again of an orchestra. Imagine if every musician tried to play the same instrument—a room full of violins wouldn't create the breathtaking sound of a symphony. The beauty and power of music lie in the diversity of instruments, each playing its part in harmony.

Remarkable teams work the same way. Many leaders fear that too many "instruments" might create chaos instead of cohesion. But the surprising truth? The most successful teams embrace the unique roles of their members, understanding that true success isn't about uniformity. It's about the harmony of diverse strengths working toward a shared and defined goal.

Or think of a winning football team (I'm talking about the American variety). It requires a remarkable coaching staff, each with clearly defined and different roles. A defensive coordinator doesn't act like a head coach. They know that a win for them looks like a turnover, a sack, an interception, a forced punt, or a turnover on downs. And if a great defensive coordinator gets promoted to head coach, they'd better know how to build an offensive strategy and assemble the right team around them.

Consider organizational teams like a mosaic. Each piece is unique and contributes to a larger, more beautiful picture.

I used to believe high-performing teams were built only of "purple unicorn" standout leaders. But here's what I've learned:

> Remarkable teams thrive by recognizing that every role, no matter how different, is essential to achieving a well-defined mission. Diverse talents and fresh ideas unlock new possibilities, but it all starts with clear roles that empower the right people to do the right things and create lasting impact on the people and communities they serve.

One of the most debated topics today in team and role dynamics is diversity, which has fueled growth and reform through Diversity, Equity, and Inclusion (DEI) initiatives. Katherine Williams Phillips of Columbia University and Charles O'Reilly of Stanford describe this in their paper "Demography and Diversity in Organizations" as heterogeneity in member attributes such as age, gender, cultural background, role, or personality traits. We'll explore this further later in the chapter.[20]

Yet, many leaders fall into the trap of trying to make every piece fit the same mold, fearing that different perspectives might slow them down or complicate decisions. But

---

[20] Williams, Katherine Y., and Charles A. O'Reilly III. "Demography and Diversity in Organizations: A Review of 40 Years of Research." *Research in Organizational Behavior*, vol. 20, 1998, pp. 77–140.

embracing unique and diverse roles is not just helpful. It's critical if you want to reach for remarkable.

Role Traps

In our work with thousands of organizations, we've observed that the most common way teams lose traction in the Roles Signature is by focusing on the wrong things. An overemphasis on harmony, an obsession with talent, or a desire for comfort and compatibility lead to misaligned roles and stunted progress.

The goal is to design roles that release the full potential of each person, so they actively contribute to the mission. Diversity of gifts and perspectives fuels energy and creativity. Trying to make every piece fit the same mold, or fearing that different perspectives might slow decisions, is not wise. We need unique roles and varied points of view to move the mission forward.

Below are three traps that pull teams off the mission. Each one can look helpful at first but quietly undermines role clarity and results.

The Echo Chamber Trap

Agreement is prized over healthy debate, limiting learning and perspective.

This shows up when teams reinforce their own ideas instead of embracing diverse perspectives. Agreement gets valued above honest feedback. People become comfortable with sameness, avoid being challenged, and settle into patterns that limit growth and creativity.

Over time innovation stalls, opportunities are missed, and perspectives become narrow. Anything worth building requires some discomfort, healthy disagreement, and a willingness to embrace the unknown.

To stay mission centered, build a culture of curiosity and openness. Invite differing opinions. Make space for constructive and even uncomfortable conversations. Seek and allow honest feedback so needed healthy conflict can surface. When debate and fresh ideas are welcomed, teams stay dynamic and aligned with the mission rather than stuck in familiar but stagnant same.

The Shiny Object Trap

Top talent is chosen without considering how well the leader fits the mission needs or the mix of gifts on the team.

This trap snares when leadership becomes obsessed with individual talent at the expense of team balance. We have all seen the rockstar Mission Savior who implodes the team because they "do not play well with others." Chasing purple unicorns, those rare and flashy individuals, often creates imbalance that hurts rather than helps.

It also shows up when leaders pursue market trends or what is working elsewhere without discernment about the unique roles on their team. What worked for them may not work for you. The new hired purple unicorn may think their old playbook is repeatable. It is not. The allure of the new and impressive can be strong, but if it does not align with your mission and the roles truly needed, you end up with misaligned expectations and wasted potential.

Instead of what looks impressive on paper, ask simple questions. Does this person complement our existing strengths? Does this move us closer to our shared goals? Evaluate new initiatives and trends through the filter of the actual roles on your team and your unique mission. Otherwise, you water down your remarkable contribution.

The Comfort Trap

Friend groups outrank strengths and role clarity, so impact stays functional.

This happens when leaders choose people for personal compatibility and comfort over diversity of strengths and perspectives. Relationships and trust are vital. But choosing people simply because they are easy to get along with, or they think like you, or they are a "good hang," will limit progress.

A remarkable team thrives on unique contributions, not just shared viewpoints. Favoring relationship over competence stifles innovation, creates blind spots, and raises deeper questions about whether the mission truly leads. This is where purpose must outrank preference.

Misaligned roles and overlapping responsibilities create unhealthy tension that slows productivity and reveals a lack of organizational clarity. This often surfaces when moving from building to scaling. To scale you move from hiring only generalists to adding specialists. Getting ahead of this means structuring roles with a growth mindset.

Leaders must shape a culture that values both collaboration and competence. Relationships should support and strengthen the mission rather than overshadow it. When diverse strengths are welcomed and every role is chosen for its impact, the team moves forward with momentum and confidence.

Keep your eyes on the prize. Resist the echo chamber by inviting real debate. Ignore the shiny object that does not fit your mission and mix of gifts. Choose capability with clarity before compatibility and comfort. Do this, and roles align. Energy rises. The mission advances.

Clarifying Each Role—One Sentence At A Time

Clarifying roles and expectations is vital when building a remarkable team. It starts with asking the powerful questions mentioned above and connects directly to your strategic plan.

A clear role description is a good starting point, but remember it is a living document—it will need to adapt to evolving needs and inevitably morph once you add an actual living, breathing person into it.

In our staffing work, we've learned that personalities and unique individual strengths don't just drive searches; they shape roles. A role description serves as an initial filter to guide your search and align a match, but true definition comes in the first six months to a year as the person grows into the role. This is where we remind ourselves that leaders are built, not bought. You don't simply find great leaders for your team (that's just the beginning); you need to develop them.

This might sound counterintuitive coming from someone who leads a staffing company. We can absolutely connect organizations with exceptional people who fit what they're looking for. However, an openness to how the mission of the organization and the mission of the leader will shape the role is essential. We've learned that a perfect 100% match doesn't exist. We can help an organization get to the 20-yard line, but they have to carry it into the end zone. This is where the real work of building and developing a leader for the mission ahead begins.

When we staff the leader of an organization, these leaders take responsibility for their own growth and development. They bring fresh leadership, vision, and sometimes even a mission shift to the organization.

Once greater clarity is established in the first year, distill the role into a one-line description, almost like a mission statement:

> "As the CEO of Slingshot Group, Tim brings vision, clarity, and direction to the work of building remarkable teams."

This is a great exercise to do personally and with your key leaders right away. It brings focus, perspective, and ownership to each role, clarifying their unique contribution for how they drive the remarkable mission forward.

A one-sentence role description also serves as a clear data point for success. It will be obvious if I'm not providing vision, clarity, and direction to the work we do building remarkable teams; that is my focus and it defines my win.

One-on-one meetings with direct reports should always circle back to this one-line description. It serves as a focal point for measuring success and defining the "win" for each role.

Effectory, one of Europe's leading employee feedback platforms, has shown through research that nearly 50% of employees across all sectors lack role clarity in the workplace. Conversely, their findings show that employees with high role clarity demonstrate:

- 86% greater effectiveness
- 84% higher retention

- 83% increased productivity
- 75% higher satisfaction with leadership

It's easy to see why role clarity is so critical and why roles are a key signature of remarkable teams. What isn't easy is defining and shaping them. But this is the best and most fulfilling work, because it's where you see people wrestle, grow, thrive, and become part of something bigger.

I used to think roles were all about harmony, finding that perfect "third" or "fifth" note in the chord (for you musicians out there). Now I realize dissonance is just as important, and often exactly what is needed to push the mission forward on the pathway to remarkable.

Barriers to Role Clarity

Silos

It's easy for silos to develop within teams and organizations and they can quickly threaten role clarity and healthy development. Roles have their greatest impact when they operate with a clear awareness of how they fit into the greater purpose and advancement of the mission.

When a silo mentality is tolerated or allowed to grow (when a team begins to operate in isolation), perspective is lost. This has a detrimental effect on growth, innovation, and the ability to work together synergistically. Silos can form out of homogeneity, when everyone thinks and works alike, or when groups rally around a shared frustration or narrow cause.

Leaders must address silos quickly and openly. These mental and relational "weeds" need to be pulled through clear, communicative efforts that encourage cross-collaboration and shared goals.

This is something we see clearly when assessing team health. When we identify silos, our priority is to help people "lift their heads up" and remember the "why." The mission that everyone is working together to move forward (see Chapter Four—Conviction). We often recommend simple steps, like asking someone outside your immediate circle for their opinion on a problem or task. Just this small act of inviting fresh perspectives can make a significant difference.

Groupthink

Another major barrier to role clarity and to unlocking the true power of uniquely defined roles is groupthink. Groupthink occurs when a team prioritizes harmony above all else, avoiding dissonance and critical debate. In this environment, consensus is valued more than rigorous thinking, which leads directly to the Echo Chamber Trap we discussed earlier.

Groupthink stifles the clarity and friction that are often needed to drive creativity and solve complex problems. Remarkable teams don't fear dissonance; they embrace it as a necessary catalyst for growth and innovation. We'll explore this in more depth in an upcoming chapter, but it's important to recognize now: clearly defined roles thrive in an environment that values both unity and healthy tension.

To address the barrier of groupthink and misaligned roles, leaders must first explore why they often resist outside input. Common reasons include fear of losing control, slowing down progress, or facing uncomfortable psychological hurdles.

Understanding the dangers of groupthink is crucial to recognizing its symptoms. Here are a few leading causes:

1. **Unchallenged leadership:** When leaders are rarely questioned, their perspectives can go unchecked, stifling innovation and accountability.

2. **Overemphasis on consensus:** When harmony is prized above honest dialogue, critical ideas are suppressed and creativity is lost.

3. **Lack of outside input or voices:** Without fresh perspectives from beyond the inner circle, teams can become insular and miss opportunities for growth.

The top antidotes to these causes include:

1. **Encourage feedback:** Create channels for honest, constructive input from all levels of the team.

2. **Welcome pushback:** Embrace disagreement as a tool to refine ideas and strengthen decisions.

3. **Seek diverse perspectives:** Actively involve people with different backgrounds, experiences, and viewpoints to enrich the team's thinking.

A Lack of Psychological Safety

This leads us to a final barrier to unlocking the power of clearly defined roles (and this list is by no means exhaustive): a lack of psychological safety.

As we discussed in Chapter 6's Key Signature: Culture, Google's extensive internal study, Project Aristotle, revealed that the most critical factor behind high-performing teams is psychological safety. This is a shared belief that team members can take risks and be vulnerable without fear of judgment, rooted in strong interpersonal relationships and trust.

On the other hand, teams lacking psychological safety do not provide an environment where clearly defined roles, and the necessary friction that comes with them, can be expressed, explored, and refined.

Teams that prioritize open communication, mutual respect, and a sense of belonging create fertile soil for role clarity. In these environments, people feel safe to step into their roles fully, contribute boldly, and challenge each other in ways that ultimately move the mission forward.

Building Your First Line of Defense

So, what is our first line of defense against the traps and barriers that dilute role clarity?

Priority #1 – Identify and Dismantle Silos

This begins with open, honest conversation. Leaders need to talk about silos openly and insist on cross-functional collaboration. When teams share perspectives and work across divisions, they rediscover their shared mission and break free from the isolating patterns that stifle growth.

Priority #2 – Celebrate Diverse and Distinct Roles

Diverse and distinct roles should not just be accepted, they should be celebrated. Highlight the differences among team members and show how those differences complement one another and move the mission forward. When people see their unique contributions as vital to the collective success, they engage more deeply and work more confidently.

Priority #3 – Create An Environment of Safety

Building psychological safety is another essential step. Encourage open dialogue and active listening to create an environment where diverse perspectives are truly valued. Look to real-world examples like Microsoft, Habitat for Humanity, The Potter's House, and Redeemer Church in

New York City, all of which have experienced remarkable results by building cultures that embrace diversity and openness.

Priority #4 – Assess Individuals Strengths

Leverage tools and frameworks to assess and utilize individual strengths effectively. Resources like Lencioni's Working Genius and Predictive Index help promote teamwork and mutual respect by highlighting complementary skills and work styles. For assessing individual suitability for a role, tools such as DISC, StrengthsFinder, and the Enneagram can provide deeper insight into alignment and personal expression.

Priority #5 – Expect and Address Resistance

Expect challenges and be proactive in overcoming resistance. Address common roadblocks such as resistance to change, unconscious bias in role assignments, and the tension between moving quickly and making thoughtful decisions. The Arbinger Institute offers excellent coaching and resources to help leaders navigate these issues. We can also learn from teams that have successfully overcome resistance, such as the team at Microsoft under the leadership of Satya Nadella. Their efforts to transform culture and embrace change arguably saved the company from slipping into irrelevance.

Priority #6 – Focus on Purpose-Based Hiring

Finally, focus on purpose-based hiring and firing rather than preference-based decisions. Role definition, driven by mission clarity, should guide every personnel move. In our extensive staffing work, we almost always identify at least one team member who needs to exit, often someone who has made more than two lateral moves within the organization. Staffing always reveals mission clarity, enabling leaders to make purpose-based decisions. Without clear roles, the search for the right candidate can quickly lose direction and derail the process.

Now, let's play some offense.

Leverage Unique Roles for Innovation and Growth

Remarkable teams don't just fill roles—they *leverage* them. When people know what they bring and how it fits, innovation follows.

Role clarity and diversity, both cognitive and demographic, fuel creativity, problem-solving, and healthy growth.

I've seen it over and over again. When a team brings together people with different experiences, perspectives, and ways of thinking, assumptions get challenged and fresh ideas rise to the surface. And as we talked about earlier, assumptions can be dangerous if left unchecked.

Remarkable teams know how to leverage diverse viewpoints to consistently outperform others. I have experienced firsthand the creative energy that emerges when teams intentionally include diverse voices at every level of the organization. This diversity can come through gender, ethnicity, education, personality type, socio-economic background, or even an individual's position on the organizational chart.

In fact, those who are willing to engage in discussion and debate when invited only increase their influence, regardless of their title or rank. Inclusion at all levels naturally leads to better decision-making and stronger adaptability.

Organizational development company Emergenetics International highlights the power of cognitive diversity within an organization. This refers to differences in opinions, worldviews, beliefs, and ways of thinking. They boldly state that cognitive diversity is critical to building a healthy culture, driving innovation and, I would add, creating role clarity. Of course, in faith-based organizations, team members must align with the overall belief system and mission. However, including people who do not think exactly like you do is essential for moving the mission forward.

Marie Unger, President of Emergenetics International, captures it well. She says, "Cognitive diversity leads to faster problem solving and to better, more innovative solutions. It also helps with overall communication. When you have a team that has diversity of thought, you have this collective of people who outperform teams that do not have a spectrum of perspectives."[21]

Their research backs this up. And this kind of growth thrives best when roles on your team are both clearly defined and intentionally diverse.

I have seen teams hit a ceiling and continue to bounce off it simply because they all think the same way and keep coming up with the same ideas.

What did Einstein supposedly say the definition of insanity is? Doing the same thing over and over and expecting different results.

Could it be that clearly defined roles that embrace diversity are the offensive play against organizational insanity?

Practical Strategies to Integrate Diverse Viewpoints

Your pathway to mission driven role definition and health can start when we implement structured frameworks that allow diverse perspectives to be integrated without causing decision paralysis. Tools like brainstorming techniques, rotating leadership responsibilities, and inviting voices from

---

[21] Brown, Aaron. "How Cognitive Diversity Impacts Employee Engagement [New Research]." *Emergenetics*, Emergenetics International, 10 Apr. 2019.

different parts of the organization to the decision making table help teams stay fresh and focused. When new voices are encouraged, teams uncover creative solutions they would otherwise miss.

Balancing efficiency with inclusion is another essential practice. This means using agile processes, effective collaboration tools, and clear communication strategies, as discussed in the previous chapter on *Culture*. It ensures every voice is heard without slowing the team down. True inclusion is not about endless discussions but about finding smart ways to move forward together.

To move from intention to action, leaders must invest in training programs, role clarity initiatives, and a strong commitment to creating an environment that genuinely values and nurtures diverse contributions. Consider this: in 2020, an estimated 2.3 million women in the United States left the workforce because organizations failed to make space for them to fulfill their roles and engage with their families.[22] The impact is unfathomable! Many organizations claim they value diversity, but few take the necessary steps to accommodate and embrace it fully.

Sustaining a culture of growth through unique roles requires more than just frameworks. It calls for nurturing a growth

----

[22] McKinsey & Company. "What We Lose When We Lose Women in the Workforce." 3 June 2021.

mindset paired with an outward focus, where individuals prioritize the needs and perspectives of others over self-interest. This encourages collaboration, accountability, empathy, and more effective role clarity. When teams continuously evolve, they become adaptable and resilient, welcoming diverse viewpoints and learning opportunities.

Measuring the impact of these efforts is critical. Using key performance indicators, regular feedback loops, and ongoing team assessments ensures that improvements are continuous. It is easy to declare diversity and role clarity as values and then move on. Before you know it you're snared back in The Echo Chamber Trap. Remember, we value what we measure. Keep measuring and revisiting role clarity and diversity to stay on track.

Recognizing and celebrating individual contributions is another powerful practice. This strengthens a culture that values uniqueness, enhances collaboration, and drives the team toward remarkable outcomes. Organizations that intentionally reward behaviors aligned with their values create environments where role clarity, organizational courage, and intentional growth thrive. Amplifying achievements and celebrating innovations that reflect core values are excellent ways to sustain this momentum.

Distinct roles not only fuel breakthrough growth but also unlock progress through discomfort and challenge. That glass ceiling that many leaders can keep bouncing off of sometimes needs a few rocks thrown at it to finally break through. Embracing distinct roles means stepping outside comfort zones and challenging long-held assumptions. Remarkable teams understand that true innovation emerges when differing perspectives push the boundaries of conventional thinking. I have seen this happen firsthand when organizations invited us to address discomfort and friction among teams. Through these experiences, we reframed that very discomfort as untapped potential that, when paired with role clarity, became a catalyst for breakthrough growth and a new level of team health.

Role clarity work in these situations is designed to create synergy through psychological safety and complementary strengths. Teams flourish when individuals feel safe to share their unique gifts without fear of judgment. As we discussed earlier, psychological safety enables open communication, trust, and collaboration, allowing complementary skills to come together seamlessly in pursuit of a shared mission. When teams leverage the synergy of distinct roles intentionally, they achieve greater efficiency, deeper innovation, and stronger alignment.

As we close this chapter, let's outline what success looks like for leaders thriving in clearly defined roles on a remarkable team.

Immediate Chemistry (and I do not mean harmony). Is this particular team member and role adding to the overall impact and organizational chemistry of the entire team?

Team Health. Is this team member and role contributing to the overall health and strength of the team?

Individual Contribution. Is this leader proficient in their role, and are they bringing added value beyond their defined responsibilities? (A leader I worked for used to say when I asked certain questions, "Well, if I knew the answer to that, I would not need you!")

Team Momentum. Is the team meeting its goals? Are there improved results because of this team member and their role?

Organizational Capacity. Does this leader and role increase overall organizational capacity and help move the mission forward?

Clarifying what the win looks like for your team means aligning each individual role with collective objectives. Every member should understand their unique contribution and how it helps achieve the mission.

I am deeply grateful for my friend who once told me what I would truly need to succeed: the right people in clearly defined roles who were different from me. So that is when I made the most powerful admission in leadership. Do you remember what it is?

Saying, "I don't know what to do next."

I would have the right people around me to help find the answer.

The only mission worth pursuing is always bigger than you. It has to be. You do not want to lead your team to mediocrity or allow your mission to become forgettable.

Leaders who reach for remarkable embrace "Scenius"—remember? The collective intelligence of the whole team while leveraging the unique roles of each member.

They're constantly asking: What's next? Who's next? How do we get unstuck? How do we move forward together?

The answers come from looking honestly at how your team works and leading with intention. When you unleash each person's uniqueness, you unlock the pathway to a remarkable team.

CHAPTER 7
SYSTEMS

SIGNATURE #5 SYSTEMS

Scalable design for remarkable growth

---

*"You do not rise to the level of your goals.
You fall to the level of your systems."*

—*James Clear*

"This is bonkers! These numbers are bonkers," I remember Sarah, our COO, saying repeatedly as she talked through her end-of-year review slide deck, which showed all the growth figures for 2021. We had achieved 54% year-over-year growth. For context, 2019 and 2020 had been steady for us despite a worldwide pandemic, but 2021 went truly bonkers.

We were energized and excited by the surge, but I was also a little nervous. It was December, and I was set to take the reins as CEO on January 1, 2022. After a 54% growth year, knowing that healthy, sustainable growth hovers around 10%, I knew this explosive surge might not last.

When I joined Slingshot nearly 11 years earlier, we were a startup. My friends were pioneering staffing and coaching in a faith-based niche market that had never outsourced this kind of work. We were scrappy and eager, determined and winsome, innovative and deeply relational. I still remember the email blast Stan and Monty sent to their network announcing the new company. I thought to myself, "I wonder if this will ever work." Soon after, two more friends joined them and suggested I might be a good fit for what they described back then as a "side hustle."

We were learning as we went, educating and persuading our market that partnering with us to build teams could be one of the best decisions a leader or board could make to move a mission forward. In those early days, landing even a few contracts each month felt incredible. I remember the simple documents and PDF contracts we created, and our early database that now feels almost laughable in its simplicity.

We started expanding our work into multiple divisions, adding division leads and new team members. Our monthly contract numbers kept rising. It was fun! There's nothing quite like starting and building something from the ground up.

In 2018, our structure and model shifted again, bringing more growth.

Suddenly we had an Executive Team, VPs, and all kinds of grown-up things that made us feel like this remarkable idea from 2007 had become a thriving company poised for even greater things. Then the pandemic hit. What now? We weathered it and then we rocketed out of it in 2021 with that "bonkers" growth Sarah described.

Then I stepped into my new role as CEO. I was honored that Monty and Stan, our Slingshot Group co-founders, trusted me to lead and guide the company that had become so dear to me and the work I believed in so deeply. I remember sitting at dinner with Monty in Nashville in November 2021, when he used his favorite car metaphor to describe what he was handing over to me:

"It's zooming down the expressway. You just need to keep the engine purring and stay in the lane and if you have the right people around you, you can focus on the road and plot the journey ahead."

I'm grateful for the momentum his empowering leadership created, and for the "race car" we built together. I'm forever thankful for his and Stan's mentorship and belief in my ability to learn, grow, and lead, which often meant just asking the right questions.

But early in 2022, the car started shuddering and shaking under the pressure of our constant speed. The temperature gauge began to creep up, the tires started slipping, and it was clear we needed to pay attention to the vehicle to keep moving forward in a healthy way. Monty's car analogy was helpful, and we took it even further by studying Jurriaan Kamer and Rini van Solingen's book Formula X that year, learning lessons from car racing (and, unexpectedly, kitchen design).

We learned that the race is rarely won on the track. It's won in the garage.

This growth season we experienced at Slingshot taught me a lot. It taught me that growth isn't always a badge of honor, it can be a warning light. Now I know that health is the goal, because without it, growth might kill you. Yes, healthy things grow, but so do weeds, and they can choke the healthy things.

That's why the most remarkable teams don't skip the "work in the garage," they focus on scalable design for remarkable growth.

And that's exactly why the next chapter centers on the fifth key signature: Systems.

> ## Key Signature #5
>
> Systems: Scalable design for
> remarkable growth.

Growth Doesn't Create Cracks, It Reveals Them

Growth can feel electric. Opportunities multiply, momentum builds, and the mission seems to open up in new ways. But growth also turns up the pressure, and pressure exposes what isn't built to last. This is where so many teams stay functional at best, not because they lack heart or talent, but because the systems that worked while building can't carry them while scaling.

For a team that's growing, the shift from building to scaling is almost always the most challenging part.

When a team is in building mode, everybody does everything. We are nimble and agile, and growth is often a surprise that feels exciting. The bar is low, and we will try almost anything to clear it. But there is a point in the life and growth cycle of an organization, especially after a season of explosive growth, when you need to shift gears to start scaling. Mindset and strategy need to change, and systems must be embraced or you will burn out before you have the chance to build out what you have learned and achieve true mission momentum.

This happened for us at Slingshot Group in 2021. We hit a tipping point and, in the excitement of rapid growth, found ourselves saying yes to nearly every opportunity. Some of that work wasn't aligned with what we should have been doing, and the strain on our team and infrastructure showed up quickly.

We had to reverse engineer the systems needed to stay healthy and protect our values, which were being stretched by our own success. The tyranny of the urgent and constant firefighting pulled us away from the real work of building the infrastructure required for sustainable growth.

There's no microwave for system development. It takes time, clarity, and adoption. Systems are what separate unhealthy growth from healthy and intentional growth.

Many well-known organizations have learned the hard way what happens when the engine of growth outruns the systems that support it.

Pan American World Airways (Pan Am) was a symbol of luxury and innovation in air travel and managed these elements well as it built its brand early last century. However, despite its early success and pioneering contributions (such as introducing the Boeing 747 to international travel), Pan Am's lack of robust systems and failure to adapt to changing market dynamics led to its decline. The airline's inability to implement effective operational and strategic frameworks contributed to its downfall, highlighting the critical importance of intentional systems in sustaining growth and success.

A similar story played out with Ansett Airlines in Australia, one of the biggest corporate failures in that country's history, which disrupted the aviation industry for years.

In today's climate, any growing organization with a remarkable mission needs systems that support these goals in order to thrive.

The System Ecosystem

If you want a picture of how systems quietly sustain remarkable impact, nature offers a stunning one. One of the most beautiful examples of systems is actually an ecosystem and happens to be a few minutes up the road from me in Colorado.

An aspen tree often appears to stand alone, but in a forest setting it's always part of a grove connected underground by a shared root system. This network allows them to share resources like water and nutrients. Essentially, it is one organism with many above-ground expressions. While an individual tree might last only a few decades, the grove can last thousands of years. When a tree becomes disconnected from the root system, it can only survive for a short time. The underground systems power the above-ground impact.

Remarkable systems are the hidden root structure that powers long-term, mission-aligned impact. When you understand that systems are the hidden root structure powering long-term, mission-aligned impact, you begin to see them everywhere.

World Vision

International aid organization World Vision is a powerful example. They have scaled relief efforts across countries and to millions of people through systems like their Emergency Management System, Integrated Strategic Planning, decentralized governance, local leadership, innovative technology, and strategic partnerships. These were not just support tools, they multiplied their mission. Their impact on child well-being and community development is unmatched not because of passion alone, but because passion was paired with intentional systems. World Vision's mission to work with the poor and oppressed to promote human transformation, seek justice, and share the good news of the Kingdom of God guided their systems to serve their deeper "why."

Churches

Massive churches such as Life.Church in Edmond, Oklahoma; Elevation Church in Charlotte, North Carolina; and Saddleback Church in Lake Forest, California demonstrate the same principle. Their multi-campus models, empowered decentralized leadership, central resources, and standardized processes enabled them to scale ministry in unprecedented ways. Mega churches that have scaled in healthy, brand-aligned ways have not wavered in their unique expressions of the mission of Jesus to make disciples.

McDonald's

McDonald's paved the way for many other successful franchise models defined by repeatable, efficient processes that allow for healthy growth aligned with mission. McDonald's became a global phenomenon not because of a single restaurant, but because of a scalable, repeatable system that delivered a consistent experience anywhere in the world. I remember the first McDonald's opening in Hobart, Tasmania, in 1989 when I was in high school. It felt like the same store you would find in California, which is exactly the point.

McDonald's use of standardized operating procedures, quality control, efficient supply chains, and performance metrics allowed them to scale in alignment with their mission to be their customers' favorite place and way to eat and drink. Systems made this possible and ensured consistency in operations, enabling efficient scaling without losing quality. While we could debate the quality of the burger all day, the success of the Golden Arches scaling model is undeniable.

System Traps

System traps are dangerous because they often look like strengths. The following traps reveal where well-intentioned teams quietly undermine sustainability, health, and future growth.

The Hero Dependence Trap

Stars carry the load because processes are thin, which leads to burnout.

This shows up when an organization leans too heavily on exceptional individuals to carry operations and uphold the mission. Top talent can fill gaps for a season, but that approach is unsustainable. Without solid systems, even the best people burn out. Efficiency declines. Talent that should be fueling the mission gets wasted fighting fires.

A superstar strategy believes that a few purple unicorns can hold everything together. It may work for a while, but it breaks at scale and over time. Even the most skilled teammates need clarity, repeatable processes, and support. Build the lane and then let stars shine inside it.

The Complacency Trap

Complacency doesn't always look like laziness; it often disguises itself as urgency. We tell ourselves we'll get to it "once things slow down," but they rarely do. The truth is, when everything feels urgent, the important quietly slips away.

Systems, culture, and leadership development often take a back seat to the crisis of the week, but those neglected priorities are the very ones that determine whether we'll be healthy tomorrow. What feels like a reasonable delay is actually a trap, because by the time we finally make room for what's most important, it's usually already costing us more than we realized.

Busyness can feel like progress, but when urgency replaces intentionality, we drift from growth toward survival. The most remarkable teams aren't just busy—they're building. They make space for what matters most, even when it's not screaming the loudest.

The Nostalgia Trap

What works today blocks what is needed for tomorrow, so quality and scale stall. Nostalgic thinking appears when teams depend on what has always worked and what seems to be working now and fail to plan for what's next. Comfortable processes meet current needs but can't carry future growth. Urgent tasks push out important improvements. Short-term wins hide long-term risk. Foundations weaken.

We need to build systems for the team of tomorrow. It's Wayne Gretzky's line: *I skate to where the puck is going to be, not where it has been.* Design for the next stage before you arrive there. Improve in small steps. Keep moving.

Old routines remain because they are familiar, not because they serve the mission. A nostalgic mindset ties teams to the phrase *"we've always done it this way."* Practices that once served the mission can become anchors. Legacy systems create inefficiencies, fail to integrate with new tools, and expose teams to unnecessary risk. Holding on because the routine is known breeds indifference toward systems and a false sense of security. Momentum slows. Alignment drifts.

Choose mission over nostalgia. Keep what still serves. Retire what does not. Familiar is not the same as effective. Remarkable teams are willing to honor the past without being held hostage by it.

System Priorities

Identifying traps is not enough. Awareness without action changes nothing.

Robust systems grow from intentionality, ongoing assessment, a willingness to change, and these priorities:

1. Conduct regular reviews of existing systems to identify needed updates or full overhauls.
2. Empower system champions who can lead development and adoption.

3. Build a culture of continuous improvement with feedback and small iterative enhancements.

4. Invest in training so people know how to use and improve the systems they own.

5. Align systems with key performance objectives so processes advance the mission and remain flexible as it evolves.

When people and systems work in harmony, exceptional individuals are supported rather than stretched thin. Teams move beyond outdated habits. The mission sits at the center of every process.

Picture it like this. Do not ask a single superstar to run the entire race carrying the baton alone. Build a well-practiced relay team with smooth handoffs and a clear lane.

Do not cling to the same old playbook because it worked before. Adapt and prepare for the next challenge. Do not rely on old blueprints that no longer fit the mission. Create new frameworks that align with your purpose today and tomorrow. Avoid hero dependence. Refuse complacency. Break the nostalgic lock. Do this and you pave the way for sustainable growth, multiplied impact, and a truly remarkable team.

We learned the necessity of establishing scalable frameworks for sustainable growth in the years following our explosive season at Slingshot in 2021. That "bonkers" season was thrilling at the time, but the fire of growth quickly became uncontained, and it got pretty hot for a while.

Many writing sessions for this book happened around my fire pit in our yard in Colorado. I love that fire, but only because it stays within the boundaries of the pit. The fire pit is the structure and system that keeps the fire healthy, hot, contained, and controlled. In the same way, organizations need strong systems to channel the energy of growth in a healthy and sustainable direction.

Investing in Systems That Empower Your Team

Strong systems not only encourage innovation but also create the foundation for long-term success. When organizations intentionally invest in these structures, they enhance both individual and collective performance while ensuring alignment with their mission and scalable goals.

Well-designed systems empower people in vital ways. They create clear structures that support both accountability and autonomy. When responsibilities are clearly defined, team members know exactly what is expected of them, which builds a strong sense of ownership.

This clarity allows individuals to take initiative and make decisions confidently, increasing motivation and productivity. Balancing autonomy with accountability means setting clear, purpose-driven commitments and providing the necessary resources and support. This gives people the freedom to determine how best to achieve goals while keeping their efforts aligned, much like a fire burning vibrantly within the boundaries of a well-built fire pit.

Systems also equip team members with the right tools and streamlined processes to work effectively. When people have access to the resources they need, from IT solutions to strong human resources support, they can focus on what matters most rather than getting bogged down by operational bottlenecks. Systems handle the essential behind-the-scenes work so that teams can dedicate their energy to the creative and strategic tasks that lead to remarkable outcomes.

Beyond this, strong systems encourage ownership. They reinforce the importance of clearly defined roles and responsibilities, supporting a culture of accountability and conviction. When individuals understand how their contributions connect to the broader mission, they feel more engaged and become proactive in reaching organizational goals.

By establishing structured expectations, leaders can confidently adopt a more hands-off approach, empowering team members to chart the best path forward within agreed-upon parameters that help move the mission forward with clarity and conviction.

Systems That Support Innovation

Developing systems that encourage experimentation and calculated risk, a Key Signature we will explore more deeply later, is vital for supporting and sustaining innovation. Strong systems provide the necessary framework for teams to experiment confidently, learn from failures, and drive meaningful progress.

One of the most powerful outcomes of these systems is that they enable creative problem-solving. When organizations intentionally create processes that support and even invite creative thinking, they become better equipped to adapt to changing environments and continuously improve. Companies like Meta and Atlassian, for example, host hackathons and innovation days, giving team members space to work on personal projects or explore new ideas. This freedom allows creativity, ownership, and a sense of shared discovery.

Remarkable organizations we have worked with often prioritize creative retreats, set aside time specifically for problem-solving, and run "pre-mortem" exercises. In these sessions, teams ask, "If we fail, why?" By anticipating challenges before they happen, they create a feedback loop that strengthens solutions in advance.

Another essential piece of an innovation-friendly system is cross-functional collaboration. Systems that intentionally bring together people from different departments and perspectives enhance the exchange of ideas and leverage diverse skill sets, often leading to unexpected and innovative solutions. Structured collaboration frameworks ensure teams work together seamlessly and prevent silos from limiting creativity.

During our team coaching sessions, we frequently encourage team members to invite colleagues they do not normally work with to help think through a challenge. The insights gained from these fresh perspectives often lead to surprising breakthroughs that would not emerge within isolated teams.

When organizations design systems that support experimentation, cross-functional collaboration, and creative thinking, they lay the groundwork for a culture that does not just respond to change but drives it forward with intention and courage.

The Financial Perspective

Budgeting for system implementation and optimization is a crucial commitment for any organization aiming to grow sustainably. Allocating financial resources to develop and maintain strong systems is not just an operational expense; it is a strategic investment that yields long-term benefits. This process begins with a comprehensive needs assessment to identify the specific requirements unique to your organization.

By understanding both current infrastructure and future growth projections, leaders can make informed decisions that align budgets with organizational priorities and maximize the return on investment (ROI).

Equally important is measuring and evaluating the return on these infrastructure and systems investments. This means looking beyond simple cost analysis to examine both tangible and intangible benefits, considering how each investment contributes to the organization's mission and ability to scale. Establishing clear metrics for ROI allows leaders to make data-driven decisions about future budgeting and system improvements.

Thoughtful investment in systems empowers teams to work more efficiently and creatively, supporting an environment where innovation can thrive.

These strategic choices not only strengthen day-to-day operations but also ensure that the organization's mission remains at the center of every decision. By investing wisely, organizations position themselves for sustainable growth, greater impact, and long-term success.

Adapting to Growth While Maintaining Mission Focus

As organizations expand, preserving the core mission becomes increasingly challenging. Remember that shift from building to scaling? It is one of the hardest turns a team can make. When an organization experiences explosive growth, there comes a point when you need to slow down, reorient your mindset and strategy, and focus on designing systems that allow you to grow without drifting away from your core purpose. Without intentional system design and strategic planning, rapid growth can lead to mission drift or even mission meltdown.

Navigating change with intentionality is essential to prevent mission drift. Growth often tempts organizations to chase new opportunities that pull them away from their original calling. Implementing systems that reinforce core values keeps expansion aligned with purpose. This might include aligning initiatives and key performance indicators with core mission objectives, designing strategy sessions that test new goals against the original mission, and assessing new ideas to weigh their potential impact versus the risk of distraction. Regularly revisiting and clearly communicating the mission keeps every team member focused on the organization's most important objectives.

Balancing the immediate demands of growth with long-term sustainability is crucial. Sustainable growth requires thoughtful planning that meets today's needs without compromising future health. This means allocating resources wisely, maintaining quality standards, and always considering the long-term impact of every decision.

Organizations also need to embrace flexibility within structure, continually refining systems based on feedback.

Listening to team members and stakeholders helps processes stay relevant and effective as the organization grows. My friend, author and leadership coach Dan Rockwell, reminds us that "crap is fertilizer." We must learn from our failures, because we know they will come, and let them enrich our growth rather than stall it.

Maintaining mission clarity during scaling is vital. Think about Airbnb. During its explosive growth from 2011 to 2015, the company remained committed to its mission "to create a world where anyone can belong anywhere." They implemented systems and strategies to maintain service quality and company culture, including trust and safety measures, quality standards like Airbnb Plus, local frameworks to maintain cultural consistency, and partnerships with cities to support sustainable growth. These initiatives highlight the importance of adaptable systems and a clear mission during rapid expansion.

Similarly, charity: water stayed true to its remarkable mission "to bring clean and safe drinking water to every person on the planet" even as it grew rapidly. They did this through systems that promoted transparency and accountability, using technology like real-time GPS tracking and satellite imaging to show donors their impact directly. Their creative fundraising approaches, such as peer-to-peer campaigns and recurring giving programs, kept supporters engaged and connected to the mission.

Practical steps for implementing mission-aligned systems start with auditing existing processes to identify misalignments. Engaging team members in this audit helps surface diverse insights and builds collective commitment to change. From there, creating an implementation roadmap with clear priorities, timelines, responsibilities, and measurable objectives guides the process forward. Measuring success is critical; teams value what leaders measure. Establishing metrics that reflect both operational efficiency and mission alignment ensures systems remain effective and responsive to change.

By thoughtfully designing and implementing systems that stay true to the mission, organizations can navigate the complexities of growth while preserving their core purpose. This approach not only supports sustainable expansion but also strengthens a resilient, healthy culture that can lead to remarkable outcomes.

At the heart of this work is stewardship. It is the responsible care and respect for your mission. Scripture reminds us, "Whoever can be trusted with little can also be trusted with much" (Luke 16:10).

We must build systems not just for the work of today but also for the growth we hope to see tomorrow. Without healthy systems, growth either will not come or will cause harm through mission drift or collapse.

Systems support consistent habits that achieve and exceed goals, creating mission momentum. Even leadership development, one of the greatest gifts you can give your team and mission, must be systematized. My friend Dave Miller, co-founder of Leadership Pathway and former Slingshot team member, frames it with a simple but vital question (in the title of his book): "Who's the next you?" The best kind of leadership is always developing those who will one day take your place.

Succession itself is a system. One we learned firsthand at Slingshot. Our co-founders modeled it beautifully. Stan would often say, "If you're growing, your role here will look different in two years." Monty modeled leadership for me and then gave me the opportunity to lead. We discovered a clear succession system: invest in culture, work on succession every day, platform emerging leaders, invest trust like a venture capitalist, and set successors up for success by designing systems with them in mind.

This brings us full circle to the "bonkers" season of December 2021 and my transition into a new role in early 2022. I learned that systems are the vitamins for an organization. Many teams call us hoping for painkillers. A quick fix or a stopgap hire. But remarkable teams know that the real solution lies in the vitamins: the slow, steady work that prepares you for healthy, sustainable growth.

Growth for its own sake can be dangerous. Consider the definition of cancer: cells dividing and growing too quickly. Unchecked growth in a healthy body can be deadly.

Ask yourself today:

> What systems currently support our mission?
>
> Where do we need to invest in more structure?
>
> How can we create frameworks that empower our team for future healthy growth?

Small changes today can have an exponential impact on tomorrow. They may be the vitamins you need to prepare for the kind of growth that leads not just to more, but to something truly remarkable.

Systems are stewardship. If you and your team can be trusted with health today, the possibilities for tomorrow can be extraordinary.

CHAPTER 8
FRICTION

CHAPTER 8

SIGNATURE #6
FRICTION

Embracing healthy conflict for growth

When the road looks rough ahead
And you're miles and miles
From your nice warm bed
You just remember what your old pal said
Boy, you've got a friend in me
Yeah, you've got a friend in me

—Randy Newman

You might find yourself humming Randy Newman's classic tune, which naturally brings to mind Woody the Cowboy, our favorite deputy, and Buzz Lightyear the astronaut headed to infinity and beyond. These two unlikely toys work through their differences to reunite with their boy, Andy, becoming BFF's in the movie *Toy Story*, where the song became synonymous.

This beloved film not only propelled Pixar into the spotlight but also revolutionized the animation industry. As of 2023, when adjusted for inflation, Toy Story (1995) has grossed approximately $738 million worldwide; a figure that reflects rising ticket prices and the changing value of money since its release.

What you may not know is that Woody and Buzz weren't the only ones navigating tension. Behind the scenes, creative differences among animators, writers, and directors created significant friction.

Disagreements over the film's tone, character development, and visual style nearly led to the project being shelved. Had it been, we would have been deprived of a heartwarming story that captured the imaginations of children and adults alike and shaped pop culture for a generation.

The road was "rough ahead" for Pixar. At the time, it was a small company with big ambitions but limited experience in feature filmmaking. The team, led by John Lasseter, was under immense pressure from Disney, the film's financier, to deliver a hit.

Tensions mounted as Disney executives pushed for a more edgy, adult-oriented tone, while Pixar's creative team, including writers like Joss Whedon and Andrew Stanton, envisioned a more heartfelt, character-driven story. This clash resulted in numerous rewrites and even a temporary shutdown when early storyboards were deemed too harsh and unlikable.

Through this creative friction, the Pixar team learned to balance their artistic vision with the commercial demands of their Disney partners. These struggles pushed them to refine the story, leading to a film that blended humor, emotion, and groundbreaking technology. The resolution of these tensions gave us Toy Story, the beloved classic that arguably launched an empire and earned cult movie status.

Back in the nineties (late last century), I was involved in several large-scale creative projects in the music industry in Australia. These experiences ranged from writing jingles and musical themes for commercial projects to pop, country, and gospel music, as well as extensive work in the children's music world. One notable outcome was writing songs for the Australian Broadcasting Corporation's national show PlaySchool and creating a kid's concept show that was sold to Warner Music Australia (though it never saw the light of day).

Around that time, The Wiggles were becoming a household name, four turtleneck-wearing rockers turned kids' entertainers, transforming children's entertainment. On multiple occasions, I've had to deny being part of their empire when revealing that writing kids' music had been a part of my journey. So, again for the record, I wasn't a Wiggle.

Through these experiences, I learned a lot about tension, and importantly, what I didn't like about it. I also learned to hold creativity and intellectual property "lightly" when working for a client who hired you to "create" to their specifications, especially if you wanted to maintain a good relationship for future business.

On the flip side, I learned when to stand my ground and fight for intellectual property that was mishandled. That's when I got introduced to intellectual property law (another story for another time) and why that kid's concept show never saw the light of day. There was redemption in that story, and it shaped my leadership in a profound way, especially in my understanding of how tension and friction play a role in breakthrough and innovation.

Sure, it's more peaceful when you're creating alone (everyone agrees with you), but can you imagine a world without the innovation that results from the fraught, friction-filled collaboration of teams? We certainly wouldn't have had Woody and Buzz teaching us about true friendship. Where would we be?

Key Signature #6

Friction: Embracing healthy conflict for growth

Don't worry if you have it, be concerned if you don't!

As a reformed people pleaser, leadership has often been a stretching road for me. Having my thinking challenged again and again was uncomfortable at first, but it ultimately reshaped how I understand tension and friction on a team.

I once believed the absence of conflict was a sign of health within a team. Now, I know it's a reason for concern.

Friction is a key signature of healthy, remarkable teams. Don't worry if you have it, be concerned if you don't!

Teams where members passionately contend for mission clarity, innovation, and diverse ideas are the teams that drive forward to great results. This is where the mission truly comes alive and evolves into all it can be. However, the line between a box office hit and a story, song, or concept that never sees the light of day can be surprisingly thin.

Friction means tension, conflict, and struggling through seemingly competing ideas. Good leaders know to allow it, not control it, though they must closely monitor it. Healthy team members enter into it with self-awareness and an open posture, showing respect for others and the mission, they are all contending for.

Again, the presence of tension in a team setting is a healthy sign. The absence of it is a cause for concern.

We all have a choice in how we engage in debate, challenge, or contention. The kind of friction we create or allow is in our hands.

Healthy tension is vital to maintaining momentum toward a mission. Unhealthy tension, however, will kill that momentum.

What does healthy friction look like?

Healthy tension is not chaos or constant conflict; it is purposeful friction that sharpens ideas, strengthens trust, and keeps the mission moving forward.

It always starts with a remarkable mission: one that people care about, are called to, and are willing to contend for. Once that mission is clear, the right people bring their unique perspectives to the table, and that's when the friction begins.

Here's what healthy friction looks like:

- When competing ideas and perspectives are expressed.
- When all voices are heard, and everyone speaks up.

- When passionate debate happens without becoming personal.

- When, despite differing opinions, everyone remains committed to the shared mission.

- When there is a leader who can make the final decision, and that leader is respected and followed.

The most remarkable teams I've worked in and with have all engaged in healthy tension. I remember being the youngest leader on a Senior Leadership Team at a large organization and learning what real tension felt like. It was during those early days, witnessing strong leadership and embracing the tension and friction that comes with healthy, passionate contending, that I learned: if you have a stall full of stallion leaders, you should expect them to kick the fence!

In my current leadership role, I have the freedom to hand-pick a Leadership Team to lead our mission-driven, Kingdom-focused work. Some of the best meetings I lead are when we are piloting, experimenting, or implementing new initiatives and contending with competing ideas about how to move forward. There's nothing more energizing than innovating and engaging with tension in healthy ways. A team and a mission are never more alive than when passionate debate is happening about new ideas, initiatives, and whether they're working, or not, and what can be learned from that.

In my work with teams over the years, I've witnessed how mission trajectory changes when healthy tension is used to solve problems and invite challenging questions, such as:

- Why have we always done it this way?
- What do we need to stop doing?
- What do we need to start doing that we haven't tried before?
- What are we tolerating?
- Who are we tolerating?

You might want to put questions like that up on the wall next time you want to engage some much-needed tension!

These questions can't be answered without creating room for healthy friction.

I think of a team I worked with that offered voluntary redundancy packages to staff in order to see who was truly on board for the right reasons. The response was surprising. It resulted in a significant reduction in staff but also became catalytic for growth and new direction.

Another organization addressed a challenging nepotism issue involving a founder's family member who was holding the mission hostage. Contending for the right way forward with the right people, and engaging in friction-filled conversations where the tension teetered between healthy and unhealthy, provided the breakthrough needed. The tough changes made were catalytic to organizational health.

This is why I'm grateful for leaders I've worked with, who taught me the right rules of engagement and showed me why friction is such an important signature of a healthy team. In executive, management, or senior leadership teams, trust must be present, and there must be opportunities to debate anything.

As I mentioned earlier, much of the friction lives in the space between healthy and unhealthy tension. It's the leader's responsibility to decide what to allow. Friction can either be a smoking gun that causes carnage on your team or a loaded slingshot that propels you forward.

The gun metaphor is easy to understand. The leader who allows friction to cross the line risks turning dysfunction into toxicity. They risk the "gun" going off and creating casualties within the team.

But think of the Old Testament Bible hero, David, and his slingshot. What if all the tension, stretching, and friction, when released in the right setting, with the right tools and the right people, propels us forward, aiming us in the right direction for growth? This could be the slingshot that moves your mission forward.

Friction Traps

What happens when leaders fail to make room for healthy friction?

In every team, tension will surface. The challenge is not whether friction exists, but whether leaders create space for it. When tension is allowed, acknowledged and addressed early, it sharpens thinking, strengthens trust, and moves the mission forward. When it is ignored or delayed, it does not disappear. It goes underground and unspoken. It starts to erode the foundations.

Avoided conflict can feel like keeping the peace, but it slowly weakens the team. Issues grow in the background. Decision making softens. Momentum slows. Over time, what could have strengthened the team begins to fracture it.

The traps that follow show how mishandled friction undermines teams and how remarkable teams choose a healthier path.

The Blindfold Trap

Leaders ignore tension, so problems grow in the dark and innovation slows.

Imagine a team where friction is ignored or downplayed. When leaders and team members fail to recognize or address conflict, the team becomes blind to the tension that is quietly brewing. Friction goes unacknowledged and unresolved. Stagnation follows. Decision making weakens. Innovation slows. Leaders who shut down, ignore, or fail to invite constructive conflict create an environment where critical voices and feedback are discouraged. This impedes growth and can lead to high turnover, dissatisfaction, and organizational dysfunction. If you notice a pattern of high staff turnover, it is often a sign that friction is being avoided and leaders are blind to it. The team's ability to move forward with clear vision is weakened.

Remarkable teams avoid the Blindfold Trap by inviting healthy pushback, asking for dissenting views, naming the real issue in the room, and treating early conflict as care for both the mission and the people who carry it.

The Harmony Trap

Polite agreement hides real concerns and silences ideas.

On the surface, harmony can look like a healthy culture. But when teams mistake surface level harmony for real collaboration, they suppress the debate that leads to better ideas. Opinions, concerns, and criticisms are withheld to maintain a façade of agreement. Leaders may prioritize smooth implementation or keeping the peace over experimentation and innovation. This suppression leads to disengagement, complacency, and stagnation. Without necessary friction, creativity and diverse thought are stifled. Big personalities dominate the conversation. The lack of real discussion results in an uninspired team that cannot push the mission forward in meaningful ways.

Remarkable teams avoid the Harmony Trap by rewarding honest feedback, making space for constructive and sometimes uncomfortable conversations, and replacing polite silence with clear discussion where ideas win on merit.

The Unspoken Influences Trap

Ghosts and elephants guide choices that no one will name, which erodes trust.

Unresolved issues or influential figures can shape decisions from the shadows. Ghosts are lingering influences from past leaders or unresolved dynamics that still direct the way choices are made. Elephants are the big unaddressed issues that everyone sees but no one will confront. Succession concerns. Nepotism. Accountability gaps. These unspoken forces create hidden friction that undermines communication and decision making. The longer they remain unnamed, the more toxic the culture becomes. Secrecy spreads. Fear grows. Side conversations replace real conversations. Trust erodes and progress stalls.

Remarkable teams avoid the Unspoken Influences Trap by bringing elephants into the open, naming what everyone senses but no one talks about, clarifying ownership, and closing the loop on what will change and when.

Navigating The Friction

I've witnessed organizations where fear dominates due to the traps associated with friction. Healthy leaders, feeling the tension, often resort to backroom gripe sessions. These private discussions lead to fractioning and splits within the team and the broader organization. Leadership challenges arise that could have been avoided by engaging in honest and healthy feedback from the start.

In multiple teams we've worked with, leaders were so feared that team members took their issues to overseers, leading to devastating interventions. These could have been avoided if the tension had been addressed directly and earlier. I suspect you've encountered similar scenarios or heard stories about them.

Please hear me clearly when I say that, sometimes, we're dealing with unhealthy or toxic leadership, and additional intervention is necessary. However, more often than not, when we deconstruct leadership wreckage, we find that the black box reveals that if healthy conflict had been engaged much earlier in the process, it could have prevented the catastrophic crash.

- Healthy friction moves the mission forward and sharpens leadership.

- Destructive conflict holds progress hostage, blurs vision, and leads to leadership shutdown.

- Healthy tension empowers team members, leading to innovation and growth.

- Unhealthy tension creates a culture of fear where great ideas remain unspoken.

- Healthy contention signals a thriving culture and open-handed leadership.

- Unhealthy friction, at its worst, leads to bullying and a toxic work environment.

As you can see, there's a lot at stake when striving for the remarkable. Woody and Buzz will tell you that the road can look rough ahead. You've got to have the stomach for it, along with the leadership intuition and self-awareness to manage it effectively. But I promise you, it plays a crucial role in driving innovation and momentum.

The late J. Richard Hackman, former Edgar Pierce Professor of Social and Organizational Psychology at Harvard University, wrote in his article titled "Six Common Misperceptions about Teamwork" that "arguments are good for a team, so long as they are handled well and focused on the team's objectives."[23]

It takes strong leadership to handle tension well and stay focused. High levels of self-awareness from the team are equally essential for self-regulation. Sometimes, the friction itself comes from courageous conversations about lack of awareness.

---

[23] Hackman, J. Richard. "Six Common Misperceptions about Teamwork." *Harvard Business Review*, 7 June 2011.

Common Categories of Friction We've Observed

1. **Directional Friction:** Conflict arises when there's disagreement around the core mission or direction of the organization.

2. **Relationship Friction:** Tension stemming from diverse perspectives or personal differences that start to affect relationships and make issues feel personal.

3. **Decision Friction:** Contentiousness around how decisions are made or who has the authority to make them.

4. **Clarity Friction:** Disagreement over the "why" behind the mission, affecting clarity around objectives, expectations, and outcomes.

5. **Momentum Friction:** Tension builds when initiatives or decisions are made but fail to move forward due to internal barriers or lack of follow-through.

Are any of these types of friction present on your team? If so, they must be addressed and handled in a healthy way to minimize wasted energy and move the mission forward. Mismanaging these types of friction can lead to disastrous outcomes.

Friction Priorities

To keep friction on the healthy side, you must have an awareness of team dynamics and how different roles and personalities interact. Prioritizing these team dynamics will help leaders engage friction wisely and keep it on the healthy side.

Priority #1 – Understand Team Dynamics

Healthy friction depends on awareness. Leaders must understand how roles, relationships, and structures shape the way tension shows up on their team. Without that awareness, friction is often misread or mishandled.

Prioritize regularly observing team interactions, naming patterns you see, and checking your assumptions before responding to tension.

Priority #2 – Pay Attention to Positional Dynamics

Leaders carry greater influence and must be especially self-aware in how they speak, react, and respond. Second-in-command leaders often feel tension first and from both directions. Those lower on the organizational chart need space to contribute with confidence, not hesitation or self-protection.

Prioritize adjusting how you listen and respond based on role, influence, and proximity to authority dynamics in the room.

Priority #3 – Acknowledge relational dynamics

Pre-existing relationships, personal history, and unresolved tension shape how conversations unfold. When left unaddressed, these dynamics quietly steer outcomes.

Prioritize naming relational history before or after key conversations so it does not drive decisions in silence.

Priority #4 – Create space for diverse voices

Teams are stronger when diverse perspectives are welcomed and heard. Without diversity of thought, background, and experience, teams drift toward agreement without depth.

Prioritize inviting input from voices that are quieter, newer, or different and ensuring they are heard before decisions are finalized.

Priority #5 – Recognize organizational dynamics

Different roles bring different priorities, and that naturally creates tension. Tenure, institutional memory, and downline impact shape how decisions are perceived.

Prioritize listening to those closest to the work and evaluating how decisions affect the team beyond the leadership table.

Two Vital Ingredients to Healthy Friction

Remarkable teams rely on two vital ingredients that lead to healthy friction: curiosity and learning.

Curiosity

Curiosity invites us to explore and understand each other's ideas and opinions. It stems from a posture of humility, admitting we don't know everything, and a desire to learn more. The breakthroughs possible from this mindset help build resilience and adaptability, which can slingshot your mission forward.

A great example of this is Amazon and how they prioritize open debate to refine ideas and strategies through principles designed to encourage critical thinking, rigorous discussion, and data-driven decision-making.

One of Amazon's top principles is: "Have Backbone; Disagree and Commit." Employees are expected to debate thoroughly, but once a decision is made, they commit fully.

This reminds me of the best organizational teams I've worked with, where friction behind closed doors tests ideas and strategies, yet in public there is clear loyalty and unified support.

Healthy friction leads to progress, growth, innovation, and creativity in every space and sector of society. Friction is a natural part of healthy collaboration when it is led and managed well. This requires cultivating an environment of trust and psychological safety. It means approaching these conversations with a proactive posture, not a reactive one.

Curiosity gives friction its right tone. It sounds like asking before assuming and exploring before defending. Here are some practical ways teams engage healthy friction with curiosity:

> Be open about it: "This may feel like criticism, but let's explore this together."
>
> Be curious: "Can I ask a contentious question?"
>
> Be committed to it: "This is too important not to play it out."

Practically, it can also mean "announcing yourself" when pushing back. Without clarity, challenging ideas can feel like a hand grenade with the pin pulled—intense and potentially destructive. Instead, announce your challenge with phrases like:

> "Here's maybe a bad idea that could lead to a good one."
>
> "Permission to give feedback?"
>
> "Can we spitball some ideas for a moment?"

I learned a lot from a leader who would challenge ideas and the status quo simply to check whether the team was still passionately committed to them. He would engage friction as a form of practice, ensuring the team stayed forward thinking and forward moving. When done strategically, this can be an effective way to maintain momentum and keep innovation alive.

Learning

Curiosity creates the posture. Learning is the outcome.

Healthy teams treat friction as a chance to grow, not a threat to manage. Learning happens when teams stay open long enough to let tension sharpen their thinking rather than shut it down.

But when things get heated and friction starts to feel unhealthy, leaders must slow the moment and lower the temperature. Learning requires emotional awareness. Phrases like these can activate a pressure release valve and help redirect the conversation:

> "I'm sensing that this conversation might be becoming unproductive. Let's take a break."
>
> "Can I repeat what I'm hearing?"
>
> "Can you help me understand where I'm struggling?"
>
> "The story I'm telling myself is . . ." (thanks to Brené Brown and others for this powerful tool.)

At this point, it might start sounding like a marriage. Interestingly, the absence of friction in a marriage often signals stagnation, apathy, and stunted growth. The same is true for teams. Where learning is valued, friction is not feared—it is welcomed as a sign that growth is still happening.

A Cautionary Tale

Many of us who grew up in the last century remember choosing movies at a Blockbuster store. At its height, Blockbuster had 9,000 stores worldwide, and it was the go-to place for home entertainment.

Now, Blockbuster is a thing of the past. It's relegated to "remember when" conversations. What happened? They failed to adjust to changing culture, technology, and habits. I also suspect there was a lack of healthy conflict on their leadership team, and they stopped moving forward.

In contrast, Netflix, which started as a DVD rental service, was able to pivot and grow. When CEO Reed Hastings recognized that streaming was the future, it sparked internal conflict. Many within the company were heavily invested in the DVD rental model. Making the shift to streaming required not only a technological overhaul but a cultural change within the company, which caused significant friction. The easier path would have been to protect what was working. Despite the resistance, Hastings pushed forward, believing that streaming would eventually dominate the entertainment industry.

That friction paid off. By 2010, Netflix fully embraced streaming and became a global powerhouse. Today, Netflix is a leader in the entertainment industry, demonstrating the power of embracing tension, change, and innovation in the face of both internal and external challenges.

Interestingly, Netflix tried to sell itself to Blockbuster in 2000, suggesting that Blockbuster take over Netflix's online operations. At that time, Netflix was a young company with big ideas, and according to Barry McCarthy, the CFO of Netflix, they were "laughed out of the meeting."[24]

At Slingshot, when debating new ideas, exploring new technologies, and trying out new ways of doing things, we often say: "We don't want to be Blockbuster."[25]

In faith based and Kingdom focused work, there is far more at stake than 9,000 video rental stores. That is why engaging healthy friction matters. It has fueled innovation across healthcare, civil rights, compassion and justice, and the arts. It has driven the creation of nonprofits that fight for the under resourced. And it has transformed churches through multi-site and multi-campus movements, turning local congregations into mission movements on an unprecedented scale.

---

[24] Randolph, Marc. "He 'Was Struggling Not to Laugh': Inside Netflix's Crazy, Doomed Meeting With Blockbuster." *Vanity Fair*, 17 Sept. 2019.

[25] Levin, Sam. "Netflix Co-Founder: 'Blockbuster Laughed at Us . . . Now There's One Left.'" *The Guardian*, 14 Sept. 2019.

We are all human, equal but wonderfully unique. When we show up as our full selves, friction is inevitable. When managed well, it deepens relationships, strengthens trust, and creates the kind of teams that truly hum together. Cue the quiet chorus of "You've got a friend in me."

Remarkable teams do not fear friction. They leverage it to create momentum. They build environments where disagreement leads to innovation, not division. Perhaps your first step is simply allowing tension instead of shutting it down. To ask, "Is there something everyone knows is there and thinks about, but no one is willing to name?"

The key to healthy conflict is not eliminating friction but recognizing and redirecting the unhealthy kind. Sometimes, it is only the presence of friction that reveals how much your mission still matters.

And occasionally, the very tension you are tempted to avoid is the thing that will propel your remarkable mission to infinity and beyond.

CHAPTER 9
RISK

SIGNATURE #7
RISK

Bold moves that drive remarkable learnings and outcomes

---

*"If the highest aim of a captain were to preserve his
ship, he would keep it in port forever."*

—*Thomas Aquinas*

Congratulations!

You've made it to the seventh and final key signature, unless you're jumping ahead to the chapters that most intrigue you (which I imagine this one would). That's okay, but I encourage you to return to the earlier chapters at some point. They build on each other and form the pathway to build remarkable teams.

This is the exciting (but scary) one! Who doesn't love risk?

Well, me! That might surprise you, considering where I'm sitting as I write this, literally on the other side of the world from the island where I started. My life has been full of risk and when I look back, nothing has ever felt truly "safe." Almost all of my major decisions have been defined by risk.

Like most people, I'm not a big fan of change, and I love comfort. I realized early on that these tendencies are in direct tension with my love of variety and adventure. That friction, when focused, led me on an incredible journey that's now spanned over thirty years and brought me here, writing about risk.

Was it my low IQ as a kid (hopefully redeemed now) that caused me to not weigh or even acknowledge the potential for failure as I stepped further out of my comfort zone? Or was it simply that, at the time, offense always seemed like the better strategy than defense when it came to making decisions?

In one of the most-watched Super Bowls in recent years, a powerhouse team came in as heavy favorites, chasing an historic (and elusive) third straight championship. They'd dominated the league for years, built on talent, confidence, and creative play-calling. But on the biggest stage, something shifted.

In my humble, unqualified opinion, it seemed the team favorite was focused more on not losing rather than winning. Their usual risk-taking, offensive style was missing. The game plan seemed to focus on stopping the opponents' running back, who had set a new NFL record for the most rushing yards in a single season. They succeeded in limiting him, but in doing so, they allowed other players to step up and take more offensive risks.

They say defense wins championships, but not without some offensive risk-taking. The underdogs took those risks. Most notably, their gutsy and risky fourth-down conversions, along with deep passing attempts. Their quarterback played a pivotal role, running, rushing, reading the defense, and calling audibles like another well-known QB (the one on the other team)! The underdogs played to win; the favorites played to not lose.

The favorites' strategy demonstrated a crucial truth: it's not the path to winning Super Bowls (and for our purposes) nor is it the path to creating remarkable teams.

> ## Key Signature #7
>
> ### Risk: Bold moves that drive remarkable learnings and outcomes

The Cost of Playing It Safe

For many organizations, risk is simply too risky when it came to moving a mission forward. But I've learned that remarkable teams embrace risk, not as reckless gambles, but as a deliberate strategy for innovation and progress.

Leaders often recognize the need for bold moves but struggle to cultivate a culture that embraces calculated risk due to the fear of failure. However, teams that understand risk as a catalyst for growth keep ambition alive, prevent stagnation, and fuel momentum toward untapped potential.

In team dynamics, risk often becomes a great paradox. Avoiding risk can, in fact, be the riskiest decision of all.

At many points in a team's lifecycle, we face a choice: play the safe card or the risk card. But often, the "safe" choice is an illusion. It can lead to stagnation, complacency, or apathy. Without risk that leads to bold action, opportunities are lost, competitors gain ground, and innovation slows. The biggest danger isn't making mistakes; it's failing to evolve and grow through strategic risk.

This is why the seventh key signature is so crucial: without risk, you won't attract the best people to your team.

Consider an ancient team that still serves as a powerful example: the disciples of Jesus. When faced with what could be considered the greatest mission opportunity of all, twelve key people left behind everything they knew to follow Jesus. This was an incredible act of risk. As a result, they became the leaders of the early church, and today, Christianity has over 2.6 billion followers worldwide—about a third of the global population. Few examples of risk have resulted in greater impact.

Today, teams starting churches in underground or secret locations in hostile countries risk their lives to advance the mission of Jesus. Even in the West, church planters take great personal risks. Some grow to become megachurches with thousands of attendees across multiple campuses, while others remain small but continue to have a significant Kingdom impact. Still, others may not survive, but their stories and lessons live on.

From these churches, organizations have emerged that have reshaped healthcare, social justice, art, and culture. All of this, sparked by strategic risk.

Embracing Risk to Lead the Way

Risk has driven technological advancements at an astonishing pace, for example, we've gone from horsepower to gas-power to electric vehicles (EVs) in a staggeringly short time span. The willingness to innovate through risk has attracted engineers and scientists eager to work on groundbreaking projects, push limits, and test new technologies in every area. It is why diseases that once wiped out generations are now combated with vaccinations. Risk in the realm of innovation has made it possible to carry unimaginable computer capability in our pockets and travel in driverless cars, all while staying connected via satellite, even in the middle of the jungle.

Risk propelled the Wright Brothers into flight, and it powered both the Soviet Space Program and NASA to reach space and land Armstrong and Aldrin on the moon. It is risk that will carry us further than we ever imagined.

SpaceX exemplifies the power of risk. The company took a massive risk by attempting what no private entity had ever done before: developing reusable rockets to lower the cost of space travel. Traditional space agencies, like NASA, discarded rockets after each launch, making space exploration prohibitively expensive. SpaceX's team spent years battling failures, including multiple crashes and unsuccessful landings, before finally achieving success in 2015. Critics labeled the idea impractical, yet the company persisted. Today, SpaceX has revolutionized the space industry, dramatically cutting launch costs and securing contracts with NASA and private entities for commercial space travel.[26]

A remarkable team takes brave and strategic risks to move the mission forward faster, stepping out in faith, embracing failure as feedback and growth, and embracing trust over fear or safety.

> Remarkable teams know that risk leads to success. This brings us to the paradox found in this Key Signature: the success achieved by taking risks is often the very thing that hinders teams from continuing to take risks.

---

[26] "SpaceX's Falcon Rocket Finally Sticks the Landing." *Wired*, 22 Dec. 2015.

Success can numb teams to the need for risk. Success is like Novocain for risk! The more successful an organization becomes, the harder it is to take strategic risks because there is more "at risk." It is why some organizations plateau or even decline.

I remember the early days of Slingshot, when we had a builder's mindset and took risks to build our business. I also recall being a seventeen-year-old musician, taking risks to convince venue owners and booking agents to let me perform for free in exchange for future work and it worked!

Now, as CEO of an established company with brand recognition and a solid track record, it is harder to take risks. Nonprofits with investor and donor confidence, and marketplace companies with shareholders weigh the risks of new initiatives carefully. Churches can also play it safe to keep from unsettling key leaders, donors, or longtime members. The desire to protect stability can quietly limit bold, mission-driven moves.

Many successful companies have ceased to exist because they did not take the necessary risks. In a previous chapter, we discussed Blockbuster's demise; a prime example of a successful company that was lulled into complacency, believing it was immune to change. Blockbuster refused to take the risk of acquiring Netflix and failed to embrace the emerging trend of streaming, clinging instead to their in-store rental model. This failure to innovate led to their downfall.

When a team experiences success, complacency often follows. Past victories create a false sense of security, making leaders hesitant to take necessary risks. Jim Collins, in *How the Mighty Fall*, describes this as the "hubris born of success" stage, where past victories lead to overconfidence and resistance to change.[27]

Remarkable teams understand that growth requires continuous challenge, even (and especially) when things are going well. They focus on defining brave and strategic risks, always balancing recklessness with paralysis. Not all risks are equal, some drive transformation, while others lead to chaos. Brave and strategic risks are calculated moves that align with vision, data, and organizational capabilities. The goal is to push boundaries without blindly gambling the future.

Google's "20% Time" policy is a great example of strategic risk-taking. Employees are encouraged to spend 20% of their work hours on passion projects, which led to innovations like Gmail and Google Maps. While not every project succeeds, Google understands that structured risk-taking fuels long-term innovation.[28]

---

[27] Collins, Jim. *How the Mighty Fall: And Why Some Companies Never Give In.* HarperBusiness, 2009.

[28] Levy, Steven. "Google Couldn't Kill 20 Percent Time Even if It Wanted To." *Wired*, 16 Aug. 2013.

Remarkable teams work out how to adjust and develop based on future changes before others see them coming. They shape their industries by "innovating around corners." They anticipate where the future is heading, take risks to get there first, and lead the way. This always requires risk, which is ironically easier for smaller, more nimble organizations with less to lose. For larger, more established organizations, staying nimble is more challenging.

In our previous example, Netflix took a huge risk by shifting from DVD rentals to streaming, redefining the entire entertainment industry. Their bold, strategic move shows that risk is not about recklessness—it's about vision and timing. Netflix, the smaller, more nimble company, succeeded, while Blockbuster did not.

But how can an established organization continue to embrace risk? This is where systems meet risk: you have to systematize it.

A great case study is Pixar's mentorship system, which promotes consistent leadership innovation. Creativity thrives on taking risks, and Pixar has made it part of its culture. Their system includes:

- Braintrust Meetings
- Peer Mentorship & Collaboration
- A Research & Development Culture
- Empowering Individual Creativity
- Long-Term Leadership Development

This mentorship-driven system has helped Pixar maintain its leadership in animation, blending technological innovation with storytelling excellence.

This is where staffing comes into play. Too often, we "play it safe" when staffing our teams, gravitating toward people who think and look like us. Taking risks with staffing means hiring for our weaknesses and adding individuals who bring fresh perspectives and innovative ideas, diversity at every level. This includes outsourcing staffing to expand your reach and possibilities, others will see what you don't see and push you to consider perspectives you would not normally entertain, because you do not want a "normal" or mediocre team.

You must prioritize and systematize listening to people at all levels of your organization—that is where the gems are mined out. Too often, we assume that the people, ideas, and strategies that got us here will get us there. This is why success can be the enemy of risk.

Risk Traps

Every remarkable mission requires risk. But unmanaged risk isn't courageous, it's careless.

When leaders become enamored by the promise of growth and success, they can lose sight of the practical limitations and challenges the team currently faces. Overcommitment follows. Stress levels rise. Setbacks mount. Even the most talented, passionate, and skilled people cannot overcome the drag of poorly assessed risk.

Without clear priorities and intentional systems, risk turns from fuel into unhealthy friction. This leads to burnout, decreased efficiency, and frustration. Untimely exits and a stalled mission are often the result.

The traps that follow reveal how teams mismanage risk and how remarkable teams learn to engage it wisely.

The Margin Trap

Ambition outpaces capacity, burning people and budgets.

Margin blindness occurs when leaders fail to accurately assess both the level of risk and the organization's capacity to handle it. In the eagerness to reach the upside, limits are overlooked and the team's bandwidth is ignored. Overextension becomes normal. Burnout happens. And the result is failure that could have been avoided.

Remarkable leaders understand that risk is not simply about taking chances. It is about knowing where the limits are and balancing ambition with reality. Yet many leaders overestimate capacity or underestimate the dangers of overextension.

Studies frequently note the gap. Most executives say innovation is critical, but very few are satisfied with the way their risk strategy actually works. In the quest for potential growth they fail to weigh both the opportunities and the challenges. The result is an unstable strategy, one that limits success and amplifies vulnerability to failure.

Margin blindness also shows up when the focus is only on the potential upside and the reality of current capacity is ignored. Push too hard without considering the bandwidth available and risk becomes reckless. The mission suffers. When everything is placed on one untested move, there is little room or margin for failure. An all or nothing mindset stifles innovation and makes adaptation difficult.

A culture that prizes experimentation and adaptability chooses incremental risks with space to adjust. When leaders push unrealistic high stakes risks without proper assessment of margin and overall bandwidth, teams lose trust in leadership and become less willing to take the smart calculated risks that build a better future.

The Impulsive Trap

Fast moves without planning or learning loops waste resources.

It is easy to mistake bold decisions for smart decisions. Impulsivity can masquerade as courage. Leaders driven by ambition and the desire for quick results jump into high stakes choices without data, strategy, or a learning loop. Resources drain. Chaos grows. The team is left overwhelmed with no clear path forward.

We have seen the pattern. WeWork under Adam Neumann pursued aggressive expansion without a sustainable revenue model or strong financial forecasting. The move looked bold. It lacked a foundation. Rapid growth imploded because there was no strategy to support such big bets. This was a classic case of overestimating capacity for growth without considering operational and financial limits. The outcome was burnout and failure.[29]

True boldness balances ambition with careful planning and the humility to learn. Build a cadence of short tests, clear metrics, and review moments. Decide. Learn. Adjust. Move again. Without that loop, impulsive bets turn into expensive lessons.

The Timing Trap

The right idea comes too soon or all at once, and execution fails.

Even the best idea will falter if the timing is wrong. When teams are overloaded beyond capacity, execution breaks down. The right risk taken at the wrong time becomes a burden. Burnout rises. Focus divides. Performance declines.

Consider Tesla's production hell during the push to mass produce the Model 3 in 2017 and 2018. Goals were bold and

---

[29] Brown, Eliot, and Maureen Farrell. *The Cult of We: WeWork, Adam Neumann, and the Great Startup Delusion.* Crown, 2021.

timelines aggressive. Supply chains bottlenecked. Workers burned out. Quality suffered. The vision was strong. Timing and execution were misaligned with the team's capabilities.[30]

Sustainable risk taking aligns bold initiatives with realistic operational capacity. Pace the work. Sequence the steps. Ensure the people, tools, and processes are ready. The right move at the right time preserves energy and improves odds. The right move at the wrong time can turn into a big, missed opportunity and a mission misaligned.

The Leadership Dilemma

It is an ongoing challenge. Leaders often find themselves caught between the need to maintain stability and the pressure to drive innovation. While stability provides a sense of security, especially after achieving a certain level of success, it can also lead to complacency. This complacency makes it difficult to adapt in fast-changing markets and environments. Innovation, on the other hand, requires risk-taking, but without careful execution, it can create disruptions that destabilize the team or organization.

Many leaders hesitate to take risks because short-term setbacks can obscure long-term gains. They fear immediate failure or difficulties, even when those challenges could

---

[30] Mitchell, Russ. "Elon Musk Says Tesla Model 3 Remains 'Deep in Production Hell.'" *Los Angeles Times*, 6 Oct. 2017.

lead to future success. Short-term issues, such as growth dips, revenue declines, or temporary inefficiencies, often overshadow the broader benefits of innovation. Remarkable teams recognize that progress often involves short-term discomfort for long-term transformation.

Take, for example, Quibi, which stands for quick bites, not the edible kind, but a short-form video streaming platform that launched in 2020. Despite receiving billions in funding, Quibi's refusal to pivot from its mobile-only content model, while platforms like YouTube, TikTok, and Netflix were already dominating the space, led to its failure. The risk they took, overengineering and under-testing a product-market fit, was the wrong kind of risk. The risk they needed to take was to learn from consumer feedback and adjust their model, but that felt too risky at the time.

This illustrates how sticking to a failing risk can actually be the bigger risk. Some leaders struggle to admit when a risk isn't working and instead double down on the original idea. This is known as the Sunk Cost Fallacy, where past investments blind leaders to the reality that a pivot or even a full stop is necessary.

Why is risk so challenging? The human brain is wired to avoid loss, which often makes leaders overly cautious in the face of uncertainty. The neuroscience of fear and failure plays a crucial role in decision-making. Fear of failure triggers stress responses similar to those caused by physical danger, leading to hesitation, doubt, and risk aversion. However, high-performing teams train themselves to reframe failure as valuable data. They use setbacks as learning experiences from which to grow, rather than seeing them as signs of defeat.

The key is recognizing when fear of failure is holding your team back. When a team consistently avoids risk, it is often a sign that fear has become the dominant decision-making factor. Leaders must assess whether hesitation is driven by rational caution or by an ingrained fear of failure that stifles progress. By prioritizing a culture of psychological safety and smart risk-taking, teams can break free from fear and pursue bold, strategic growth. Leaders can break through this leadership dilemma and reshape their perspective because:

Remarkable Teams See Risk Differently

Remarkable teams don't see risk as a threat but as a tool for innovation and progress. They understand that calculated risk drives transformation, while avoiding risk leads to stagnation. The key is distinguishing between reckless gambles, which lack strategy, and strategic bets, which are grounded in vision and data.

Obviously not all risks are created equal. The most successful teams differentiate between reckless gambles and strategic bets:

Type of Risk	Characteristics	Examples
Reckless Gamble	• No clear strategy • High risk, low control • Based on gut feeling rather than data • Vision without resources • Wrong timing • Too aggressive	• **Quibi's failed streaming service** (launched with a $1.75B investment but without proper audience research) • **WeWork's aggressive expansion** (Lacked a sustainable revenue model or strong financial forecasting) • **Tesla's efforts to mass produce the Model 3 in 2017 and 2018** (Goals were too bold, timelines too aggressive, supply chain and workers couldn't keep up and quality suffered)

Type of Risk	Characteristics	Examples
Strategic Bet	• Grounded in vision, data, and resources • Thoughtfully calculated • Pushes boundaries without endangering the organization • Mission aligned	• **Netflix shifting from DVDs to streaming** (short-term losses but long-term transformation) • **YouVersion's (by Life.Church) bold bet on technology to scale the Bible.** (Invested in an untested digital product to now be one of the most influential digital ministry tools ever) • **Space X's Reusable Rockets Strategy** (Leveraged costly experimentation and failure for ultimate market shaping success)

The Risk Equation

Bold moves are not based on gut instinct alone; they are calculated decisions that balance big-picture vision with solid data. Fear can distort risk assessment and lead to either hesitation or impulsiveness but should not be ignored. By framing risk through the lenses of vision and data, teams can inform their fears and make decisions that push boundaries without gambling the future.

Making bold moves is not about relying solely on instinct. It's about thoughtful decision-making. Fear can distort risk assessment, leading either to paralysis (overcautious leadership) or recklessness (acting without strategy).

To manage this, high-performing teams apply a Risk Equation to frame decision-making:

(Vision x Data) ÷ Fear = Strategic Boldness

VISION: Does this risk align with long-term goals? Does it push us forward meaningfully?

DATA: What evidence supports the likelihood of success? Have we tested this idea incrementally?

FEAR: Are we holding back due to fear of failure, or are we rushing in due to fear of missing out?

SpaceX gives us a great example of how this risk equation can play out. The goal for SpaceX of making space travel affordable (Vision) was paired with years of engineering, testing, and research (Data). However, early failures (Fear) could have derailed SpaceX if they had not methodically balanced their risk-taking approach.

We absolutely need to reach for the stars (pun intended) with our remarkable mission's vision, but we also need to do the work on the ground, learn from our mistakes, and continue moving forward and upwards.

Building a Risk-Ready Culture

The greatest danger for any organization is not failure but stagnation. Avoiding stagnation means turning short-term pain into long-term transformation.

Many of the most successful companies or organizations took risks that involved short-term setbacks for long-term gains, whether it was Netflix shifting to streaming or Apple betting on the iPhone. Even a mission-driven nonprofit might chase an initiative that risks current donor support but could attract a whole new audience or donor base. Scenario planning helps mitigate unnecessary exposure while ensuring that risks are aligned with growth.

To innovate, teams must feel empowered and encouraged to take smart risks without fear of punishment for failure. A "Failure Budget" gives teams permission to experiment, learn, and iterate without unnecessary consequences. When leaders create an environment where strategic risk is encouraged, teams move faster, smarter, fail forward, and push toward breakthrough success.[31]

A Failure Budget is a set amount of time, resources, or funding allocated for high-risk, high-reward experimentation. Here are the outcomes:

- Encourages teams to test bold ideas
- Normalizes smart failure as part of progress
- Prevents reckless risk-taking by defining boundaries

Remember Google allows employees to dedicate 20% of their time to experimental projects, even if they go nowhere or fail. This approach led to products that transformed the company.

The scenario we discussed in the previous chapter with the movie Toy Story was likely a result of Pixar allocating resources for risky storytelling concepts. Inside Out, for instance, was initially considered too abstract. Pixar's willingness to "fail fast" in early stages enabled it to produce high-quality films without fear of catastrophic failure.

---

[31] Pasricha, Neil. *You Are Awesome: How to Navigate Change, Wrestle with Failure, and Live an Intentional Life.* Gallery Books, 2019.

Leaders need the freedom to fail because that's often where the gold is discovered. Without that freedom, risk is often weaponized. You don't want a team that prioritizes avoiding mistakes!

Back to the wisdom of rockers: Bono, from U2, said, "My heroes are the ones who survived doing it wrong, who made mistakes, but recovered from them."

Playing offense, not defense, is how new ideas happen. Many amazing things have been discovered by accident (such as chocolate chip cookies, potato chips, Silly Putty, and Post-it notes!). Failure as a result of taking risks can actually lead to innovation.

Are you allowing freedom to fail? If not, you're likely not taking risks.

Here are three immediate ways you can implement a failure budget:

1. **Set clear guidelines** – Define which areas are open for risk-taking.

2. **Allocate resources** – Dedicate time or money for experimentation.

3. **Measure learning, not just success** – Evaluate insights gained from failure.

Risk Priorities

Remarkable leaders handle risk differently. Here's what they practice when leading through risk:

Priority #1 – Reframe Setbacks

These leaders remind their teams that short-term challenges fuel long-term success and often pave the way for future breakthroughs. Temporary struggles, such as lost revenue, failed experiments, or internal resistance, can disguise the real value of innovation and change. The key is to focus on long-term gains and use setbacks as learning experiences rather than signs of defeat.

Priority #2 – Conduct "Pre-Mortems"

Leaders should spend time asking, brainstorming, and whiteboarding the question: "If we take this risk and fail, why did we fail?"

Listing possible scenarios for failure will help identify early signs and avoid potential pitfalls. Create a risk-taking framework that aligns with your mission:

For example:

- We take risks that are _____.
- We filter initiatives through our mission which is _____.

- We don't just take the safe and easy option.
- Is this initiative: Aligned, Bold, Considered, Prayed over, Worth it?

Priority #3 – Be Mindful of the Science of Fear

Remember, the brain can work against smart risk-taking because it is hardwired to avoid loss. Studies have shown that leaders are naturally hesitant to embrace uncertainty, and fear of failure triggers stress responses that lead to over-caution or inaction. This often prevents teams from making bold yet necessary moves.

Remarkable teams train themselves to see failure as data, "crap as fertilizer," using setbacks as stepping stones to refine strategies and push forward. People fear losing twice as much as they enjoy winning, meaning leaders often avoid risk even when the potential rewards are far greater. Uncertainty triggers the brain's amygdala (the fear center), activating a fight-or-flight response that discourages bold decision-making.

Priority #4 – Break Free from Fear

Recognizing when fear is holding your team back is crucial. When a team resists change, it's often a sign that fear has overtaken ambition. Leaders must assess whether caution is strategic or simply driven by fear of failure, which can paralyze progress. By prioritizing psychological safety and encouraging a culture of intelligent risk-taking, teams can build the confidence needed to embrace bold, forward-moving decisions.

Priority #5 – Facilitate a Risk-Ready Mindset

Our job as leaders of remarkable teams is to cultivate a risk-ready mindset, making risk a continuous practice rather than a one-time event. This ongoing discipline keeps teams agile and ahead of the curve. Regular risk reviews, post-mortems, and adaptability exercises help teams fine-tune their approach, learning from past experiences while preparing for future challenges. By continually assessing and refining their risk culture, teams can remain innovative, resilient, and moving forward.

Dare to Take Smart Risks

All of our key signatures build upon and support one another. You can't take risks if you don't have conviction, a clear message, a healthy culture, defined roles, good systems, and the friction to test the risk before you take it.

When I think back over my journey and how a seemingly risk-averse person's life has been marked by so much risk, I can only point back to psychological safety.

While I've sometimes questioned my choices and decisions, I've never questioned my self-worth. You can't take risks without a strong sense of who you are and the freedom to be fully yourself. For me, this points back to my family of origin and the healthy love and boundaries I received as a child.

I was raised to believe that anything was possible, that my responsibility was to leave my corner of the world better than I found it, and to stay "Kingdom aligned." But no matter what, I would always be loved. That foundation allows an individual to take risks in a more fearless way.

I remember sending an email to my parents on the twentieth anniversary of leaving home. I wrote:

> **From: Tim Foot**
> **Sent: Wednesday, 6 February 2013**
> **To: Greg Foot; Anne Foot**
> **Subject: 20 years ago . . .**
>
> . . . today I began an adventure by moving to Sydney and giving ministry and music a try! Remember?
>
> Thanks for your belief in me and your support, which made me think anything was possible!
>
> Love you both, even though I probably won't be moving back . . .
>
> xx

My dad replied:

> I knew it was around this time but wasn't sure of the exact date.

All I'd say is that God's hand has obviously been upon you as you picked up the ball that was lying in front of you and ran with it.

I guess there's a heap of things you could have done with your life, but I can't think of any that's better than what you're doing right now and have done over the past 20 years.

I wonder what the next 20 years will bring as you continue running towards the end zone!

Hopefully, we'll both still be here to love and support you as we've always done.

xx

Well, I'm over halfway into that next twenty and halfway around the world from where I started. They are still loving and supporting me as I run toward the end zone, taking risks as I go.

The future belongs to those who dare to take smart risks. It is the fuel that propels us forward. The most remarkable teams are those that embrace uncertainty, take strategic risks, and continually push toward unreached potential. They don't see risk as something to be feared, but as a necessary ingredient for growth, innovation, and industry leadership.

The organizations that will thrive in the future are not the ones that play it safe, but the ones that dare to make bold, calculated moves in pursuit of their remarkable mission.

CHAPTER 10
TEAM AWARENESS

TEAM AWARENESS

Putting the 7 Key Signatures Together for Team Momentum

"A goal without a plan is a wish.
Momentum is built on execution."

—*Herm Edwards*

As we've looked at teams that have moved beyond being simply functional and have truly reached for the remarkable, we've seen a consistent pathway emerge.

Remarkable talent is not enough.
Remarkable effort is not enough.
Even a remarkable mission is not enough.

To reach for the remarkable, it's going to take a remarkable team that is aligned around the seven key signatures.

Conviction, Message, Culture, Roles, Systems, Friction, and Risk are not abstract ideas. They are lived realities that shape whether a team merely survives or actually makes a difference.

We have seen this tension play out in story after story. From aviation to technology, music to film, and sport to organizational leadership, the same pattern emerges.

In every one of these stories, there were countless others who started in the same place. For Steve Jobs and Steve Wozniak working in a garage, there were thousands of inventors who stayed there. For Jerry Seinfeld and Larry David and their comedy pilot about nothing, there were thousands of ideas that never made it to a screen. For Bob Pierce's vision to confront poverty and injustice, there were countless equally sincere efforts that never moved beyond intention. And for four Irish musicians who you could say started as a "garage band" and became U2, there were scores of other bands who never left the garage.

As we come to the final stretch of this journey, the question sharpens. It is no longer whether the Seven Key Signatures matter. The question is whether your team is experiencing them together in a way that creates momentum and sustains impact.

And yet, this is where many teams quietly stall.

Not because they reject the Seven Key Signatures, but because they assume alignment without ever verifying it. Leaders often believe that clarity at the top automatically translates into clarity across the team. They feel conviction deeply, communicate a message consistently, value culture sincerely, and trust the systems they helped build. From their vantage point, the pieces seem to be in place. But what is clear to one is not always shared by all.

This is where the gap emerges.

Teams rarely break down because they lack vision or values. More often, they lose momentum because they lack awareness of how those values and ideas are actually being experienced together as a team.

What leaders intend or assume and what teams experience can quietly drift apart. Conviction feels strong in the boardroom, but unclear on the ground. The message sounds consistent in planning meetings, but mixed in daily execution. Culture is described one way, while lived another. Roles are assumed rather than understood. Systems that once served the mission begin to slow it. Friction is avoided instead of stewarded. Risk is carried by a few instead of owned by the whole.

None of this happens overnight. It happens gradually, subtly, and often unintentionally.

That's why I see the biggest barrier holding teams back is not self-awareness, it's team awareness.

Team awareness is the discipline of seeing the team clearly, together. It is the ability to understand not just what you believe is true, but how the team is actually experiencing conviction, message, culture, roles, systems, friction, and risk in real time. It is what allows teams to tune themselves before they drift out of rhythm. Without it, even strong teams slowly lose momentum. With it, teams gain the clarity needed to move forward with confidence.

The Team Awareness Assessment

You can't have a remarkable team without team awareness.

That's why we've created a simple and practical tool: the **Team Awareness Assessment**.

This assessment provides leaders with a clear picture of how their team is functioning across the Seven Key Signatures.

The Team Awareness Assessment is not complicated or overwhelming. It is straightforward and designed to give you insights that highlight strengths and pinpoint areas needing refinement. This can lead to strategic priorities, greater clarity, helpful next steps and team awareness across all of the seven key signatures to know where you are:

Unhealthy → Inconsistent → Functional → Remarkable

The results from this assessment will have a monumental impact on what you point your focus and energy towards.

Think of it like notes on a conductor's score, allowing leaders to recognize where the notes align beautifully and where dissonance is occurring so you can build toward a crescendo of impact.

Or think of it like the check engine light on a car. You may sense that something isn't working quite right. Without diagnostic tools, you are left guessing where to focus your attention. The Team Awareness Assessment does that diagnostic work for you. It moves leaders from vague concern to clear insight, helping identify what actually needs attention. It helps ensure long-term effectiveness, resilience, and impact for the mission that matters most.

> **You can access the free assessment at ReachingForRemarkable.com.**

Momentum

What you've hopefully learned from this book is that simply paying attention to the seven key signatures won't guarantee that your team is remarkable (that's why we've identified the traps). But I can guarantee that without these signatures, your team will struggle to sustain remarkable momentum.

Wouldn't it be nice if there was a guaranteed formula for making your team remarkable just by following our seven focus areas? While we can't promise instant success, what we can guarantee is that these seven signatures, when followed and focused on, will form a pathway to momentum: a precursor to remarkable.

Sometimes, momentum can feel elusive, like a mirage in the desert. The truth is, this often happens when we fall into a pattern that keeps us stuck, or when one of these key signatures becomes a problem area. When momentum is lacking, it's a signal to review the seven key areas and identify any trouble spots that need attention.

How to Recognize Momentum

How do we even know when we have momentum? How do we begin to harness it? How do we recognize the "strength or force gained by" organizational wins and forward motion? Often, momentum can be overlooked, and we totally miss the wave of opportunity.

Back in the early days of Slingshot, we used the "ride the wave" metaphor to drive goal achievement (perhaps it had something to do with our origins in California). We've experienced times of incredible momentum when we've caught the proverbial big one and surfed it to the beach. Other times, we've been paddling hard to just catch the swell. It's all part of the ebb and flow of organizational life. The tide comes in and goes out on its own schedule, but we know it will come in, and it will go out. So, we take advantage of those unpredictable rhythms.

But you always know when you've caught the wave! What does that look like for your team?

We know we have momentum when:

- Everyone is taking ownership and contributing. Team members are aligned with the mission and actively working toward it.

- Our Team Awarness Assessment results are encouarging! Everyone understands what's important and is paying attention to it.

- Focus equals growth. The work is purposeful and produces results. It's good work, not just "busy" work.

- You're being imitated because you've created new paths that are shaping your space.

Understanding Momentum vs. Productivity

So, how do you know when you have momentum? The unhelpful but legitimate answer for those who know is: you just know, you're riding the wave!

Like the tides, there are natural organizational rhythms that healthy, functional teams can harness to catch the wind of momentum toward remarkable. There are times like leadership transitions or the honeymoon period for a new leader, certain times of the year, or specific work cycles that provide opportunities for natural momentum. Social, political, and cultural moments can also surprise us with momentum waves, depending on the space we operate in.

Great leaders and remarkable teams can often predict these and take advantage of them.

However, momentum is often confused with functional productivity. You can be making progress, meeting goals, and working as part of a competent, efficient, and proficient team. You might feel like the team is healthy and operating at a consistently high level of output. This can all feel like momentum, but there may still be a lack of maximization or true momentum. At the end of the day, you're moving forward, but not necessarily "winning." You catch the wave for a moment but don't ride it all the way.

What Drives Momentum?

As you assess your team's health in these seven key signatures, ask a deeper question. What extra element could connect our team to something larger than ourselves? What goal would stretch us into heartfelt cooperation rather than functional coordination? What would push us toward the edge of our potential together?

Remarkable teams do not drift into greatness. They change the world they touch. They pioneer new ground as market leaders. They innovate new ideas. They set direction for others. They redefine what is possible.

We also remember an earlier lesson.

Winning is not everything. Often the most important learning happens in seasons of loss or setback. When we look for patterns in those seasons and learn from them, we prepare ourselves for the next wave of momentum. Like cleaning up the beach when the tide is out, we get ready for what is coming.

In the end, if your team aligns around a clear mission and takes the seven key signatures seriously, you will place yourself on the path toward momentum. The warning is simple. Do not mistake productive functionality for momentum. If you suspect that you have confused the two, look at the other teams around you for context and perspective. It might be time for a reset. Time to take the assessment. Time to engage some healthy friction or embrace a new strategic risk. Time to rebuild some heartfelt cooperation.

Then, when the swell rises, you will be ready to catch the wave and ride your way to remarkable.

Building and sustaining momentum can be challenging for any team, but when fueled by a remarkable mission, the impact can be both significant and redemptive. It's like an orchestra that goes from individually "tuning up" to that one transcendent note at the command of the conductor's baton that swells and becomes the overture before the masterpiece. The marks of remarkable are these seven key signatures that form the pathway to realize extraordinary potential.

Years ago, when my oldest son was starting middle school, he was required to choose an instrument. Saxophone was the surprising pick for a kid whose gifts were clearly on the athletic field. We enrolled him in a two-day summer music camp for incoming orchestra students. A crash course in how to care for their instrument, make a sound, follow a conductor's cues ("tacet" being my favorite), and read basic music.

On the final afternoon, parents were invited to witness the grand debut. We crowded into the back of the room, holding our breath as the conductor raised her baton. Awkward pre-teens lifted their shiny new instruments in unison, the baton came down, and . . . chaos. An indescribable storm of squeaks, shrieks, booms, and bangs, all gloriously out of time.

A fellow dad leaned over, grinning with equal parts hope and disbelief, and whispered, "I think they've got it!"

By the end of that year, under the guidance of a first-year teacher who would go on to win "Best New Teacher in the District," they truly did. She had taken a roomful of unpolished individuals, aligned their focus, taught them to listen to one another, and shaped them into a single harmonious whole. That's the work of building a remarkable team; turning initial noise into music that moves the mission forward.

Important work is never easy work, and those called to it should not be surprised to face significant challenges along the way. For those of us building teams, reaching for remarkable is both the call and the destination. With that call comes the certainty of significant challenges and a commitment to walk with intentionality, trust, and a shared commitment to the mission through the highs and lows of teamwork. This starts from the very first imperfect note.

These Seven Signatures, when monitored and focused on closely by your team, provide the pathway needed that can change the cacophony of noise into a harmonic note for your organization and team. They point the way to healthier collaboration, more effective leadership, and greater impact. As we have explored throughout this book, these Seven Key Signatures—Conviction, Message, Culture, Roles, Systems, Friction, and Risk—are not just lofty ideas. They are practical building blocks that can transform how a team approaches and advances its mission with sustained impact.

These building blocks provide a pathway for your remarkable mission to be powered by the remarkable team it deserves. They give teams a framework to play in tune, in time, in rhythm, embracing momentum and nuance while reflecting the heart of the mission. We have seen in story after story that the power of teams intentionally committed to these focus areas realize so much more potential than what could be achieved individually.

Remember Brian Eno's "Scenius" in chapter 6: the intelligence of a whole group of people. Now add the power of our seven signatures to a higher calling and a vision of flourishing, both individually and as part of a team, and the results can be nothing short of remarkable. Key Signatures matter.

Building and leading toward these key focus areas not only gives an organization a much better chance of succeeding in the tasks and projects on their agenda, but also of succeeding long-term in creating environments where the mission is lived out in ways that create lasting change in the lives and communities they serve.

The work that we have been covering in this book has exponential impact. As we now turn to the tools and strategies for assessing team health and accelerating growth, it is worth pausing to remember that the Seven Key Signatures are a blueprint for mission-driven impact. They are a way for a team to move beyond just surviving, to truly thriving in ways that reflect the heart of the mission and do the hard work of advancing it together.

The work we do is more than just about seeking success. Success is good, but it's not the finish line. True fulfillment comes when success moves toward significance—when we build teams that are aligned with a greater mission, that reflect unity, purpose, and achieve exponential impact that outlasts us.

The Path to Remarkable Teams

We've come to the end of our journey through the seven Key Signatures of Remarkable Teams.

I hope you have been inspired and challenged as we have explored the ways we are called to achieve more together and strive for greatness.

My greatest hope is that these key signatures continue to scale and multiply our efforts and how we lead.

Building teams takes time and intentionality. It takes trust. It takes people committed to a shared remarkable mission and to working together. It takes putting people ahead of agendas and ego. When we do this and focus on the right key things, we can build teams that are unified, courageous, skilled, and unafraid of hard work and sacrifice.

You have a remarkable mission that can change the world. It may be just your corner of the world or your particular space, movement, or industry, but it matters. It matters so much that your most critical and important focus should be the key signatures that guide your team. If applied, these seven will lead your team to health, aim you forward, and catapult your mission.

Let's do this.
Let's build this.
Let's stay curious and reach for remarkable.

CONCLUSION

Conclusion

THE TEAM I SEE

What's the best concert you've ever been to?

That's one of my favorite "go to" questions.

Usually, I break the rules when the question gets reversed and I come up with two or three answers because I love live performances. The anticipation of the opening, the lighting, the haze, the orchestra warming up. Then, we get to witness the dynamics of a remarkable team unfold before our eyes.

Likewise, in a sports team win—especially in a championship game—you watch the winning team accomplish their mission through remarkable feats.

Something superhuman happens when teams work together. I've heard stories of sick band or cast members who, otherwise unable to walk to the bathroom, still get through a show for the sake of (and powered by) the rest of the team.

I still remember witnessing Aussie rules football great Anthony Stevens playing in the '99 Grand Final (for my beloved Kangaroos) on a fractured foot!

Or Michael Jordan scoring 38 points during the 1997 NBA Finals while battling severe food poisoning (sometimes unable to stand) and hitting the game-winning three-pointer to lead the Chicago Bulls to victory over the Utah Jazz.

Also legendary is Jack Youngblood, who played the entire NFL playoff season (including helping the Los Angeles Rams win Super Bowl XIV in 1979) with a fractured fibula!

Teams are powerful, and when healthy and harmonized, they can achieve remarkable things together, lifting each member to exceed their best and move beyond their brokenness.

We are in an age of unprecedented leadership burnout and breakdown. We're isolating ourselves, trying to shoulder too much on our own and stalling and restricting mission impact.

Now, more than ever, we need teams to work, thrive, and harmonize.

When we work together, we make a collective difference—one that literally makes the world a better place. I see that world. I see that team. Can you?

The team I see complements each other's strengths and compensates for each other's weaknesses. They celebrate differences and experience increased impact.

They urge the world to do better and be inspired.

I want to be part of that team!

The team I see is curious. They listen and learn from each other and those they serve. Their "why," purpose, and mission are communicated in both big and small ways, in everything they do and say and in how they're experienced.

They define and refine who they are every time they approach a situation with unassumed knowledge.

They show the world that curiosity makes us all better.

I want to learn on a team like that!

The team I see has "healthy soil." Shared resources that promote growth. The right leaders thrive on this team and contribute nutrients back into the culture. This team doesn't take growth for granted or get distracted by weeds; they pull them while continuing to nourish and water the core.

They remind the world that together we can all win.

I want to grow on that team.

The team I see genuinely cares about each other. They realize this is a force for growth and impact like no other. They value the person in front of them, knowing that the results of this impact scale exponentially.

They make the world a better place.

I want to belong to a team like that!

The team I see is moving forward, which means they embrace friction and tension. They realize that holding things loosely and engaging respectfully is better than stalling out or losing ground.

They are honest, open, and thoughtful. They are also passionate, protective, and resourceful.

They remind the world that it's okay, and actually healthy, to disagree, because this leads to progress.

I want to journey together on that team!

The team I see is collectively brave. They draw on the strength of each other and the sum of their strength and experience. There is room and trust to ask tough questions, do hard things, and innovate new ideas. There is no detail too small to ignore and no dream too big to consider.

They remind the world that anything is possible.

I want to be courageous on a team like that!

The team I see uncaps its potential by inviting different and diverse voices to speak into direction, culture, evaluation, and mission momentum. There are new thoughts and ideas that promote buy-in and commitment at every level.

They remind the world that every voice matters.

I want to contribute to a team like that!

Do you see this team?

Do you recognize the signatures that mark and define them?

But they're not just characteristics and values. They're ultimately something far more remarkable.

My friend Betty told me of a small-town five-and-dime store in the 1960s, unlike any other. She would frequent the store with her young daughter and son, and the store owner and his wife would greet them at the door, gather the kids, and engage Betty in all kinds of conversation about life and the times . . . It was a different day.

On one such visit, the idea of opening a second store was discussed, and Betty joked about franchising and expanding to the "big smoke."

"That's not my dream," the store owner replied. "My dream," (or dare I call it his mission), "is to simply offer quality products at affordable prices for everyone."

He opened a second store in the neighboring town where Betty lived. Soon after, he expanded that store into what was described as a retail phenomenon. On one particular trip, as he carried Betty's groceries out to her car, she asked him what the key to his success was. This prompted him to ask for Betty's keys as they approached her car, holding them up and saying:

"These are the keys to my success." He continued, "I may have the key to the store, but my customers have the keys to my business, and without them, I have nothing."

Betty's adult kids still talk about those visits to this day, reminiscing about the store owner "Mr. Sam." The world knows that visionary as Sam Walton. I wonder what he would make of the empire now known as Walmart if he were alive today. Or Walmart's evolved mission statement: "To save people money so they can live better."

Sam knew that the most remarkable key signatures are people.

The first step to your remarkable team is remembering that it's about people.

Shakespeare wrote, "We are such stuff as dreams are made on."

We. Not me.

Your key signatures start with the uniqueness illustrated in the signatures of each of the people on your team. They are a gift to be discovered and known, listened to and cultivated, cared for and contended for, trusted and included.

If you're ready to embrace the team you've been given to live out the mission that's your unique vision, the orchestra could be tuning up for you to harmonize in ways you've never experienced before.

Because every remarkable mission needs a remarkable team.

ACKNOWLEDGEMENTS

To my remarkable team at Slingshot Group, *thank you* for the daily privilege of learning alongside you. You sharpen me, strengthen me, and model what it looks like to reach *together*. I am deeply honored to do this work with you.

Mum and Dad. *Thank you* for always being there to love and support me, and for instilling in me the belief that remarkable is both possible and worth reaching for.

To my two boys Joey and Jacob. Over the years, as I've sat as a proud dad on bleachers, courtside, and at the field, you've inspired me in real time with what teams are capable of and what's possible when skill, talent, focus, and hard work come together. Know that I'll always love you regardless of the final score and long after you hang up the cleats. Thanks for putting up with all the hours of me writing "Dad's book."

And last, but never least, Mandy. You are my first and most important teammate. Without you, this adventure across the world would likely never have happened, and if it had, it would have been unremarkable. I couldn't do this without you, and I wouldn't want to. *Forever grateful* that it's WE and not just me.

www.ingramcontent.com/pod-product-compliance
Lightning Source LLC
Chambersburg PA
CBHW071712170526
45165CB00005B/1980